Encounters

with

R.S.

Encounters with R.S.
R.S. Thomas at 100

Edited by John Barnie

with a Foreword by Ali Anwar

The H'mm Foundation

Cover photographs of R.S. Thomas © Bernard Mitchell 2013

ISBN: 978-0-9927560-0-0

Acknowledgement is due to Gwydion Thomas and Kunjana Thomas for permission to quote from the poetry of R.S. Thomas in the essay by Barry Morgan.

Typeset and designed by Dafydd Prys
Printed in Wales by Gwasg Gomer, Llandysul

Published by The H'mm Foundation, c/o Bevan and Buckland, Langdon House, Langdon Road, Swansea Waterfront, Swansea SA1 8QY

Contents

Foreword

Ali Anwar

I'm delighted to provide a Foreword to this collection of memoir-essays on my favourite poet, R.S. Thomas, which is published by the H'mm Foundation during the centennial celebrations of his birth.

Seeing my name among the list of prominent contributors makes me feel that I'm the odd one out, for I never had the pleasure of meeting R.S. Thomas, or of studying and writing about his work. What I do have in common with them, however, is an immense admiration for this great Welsh poet.

I am a businessman, living in Cardiff, working closely with a variety of poets, writers, musicians, and business and community leaders, to bridge the gap between poets and the public by showcasing poetry in the workplace, and developing innovative ways of giving poetry a higher profile in people's lives.

Building links between the business and the arts communities should be a creative experience for both, especially in a country which has a deep and innate respect for poetry. It should also be a new source of income for poets, and hopefully a source of inspiration for people in business. The present publication is one result of this project.

'I came for a day / setlo am oes' (stayed a lifetime). This piece of 'municipal graffiti' on the wall of a housing association block in Christina Street, Swansea, written by the poet Nigel Jenkins, speaks poignantly of my own situation since my arrival in 1977 from Baghdad. Expecting to spend only a few days in Wales, a place I didn't know, I bought a return ticket. I still haven't used the return part.

My personal story as an 'accidental incomer' is too long to tell, but yes, I fell in love with Swansea, that 'ugly, lovely, town', as Dylan Thomas put it, and have been happily settled in south Wales for over thirty years.

I found R.S. Thomas's poetry most interesting, particularly his poems that engage with politics. Four years ago the poet Grahame

Davies helped me gain access to some archival material on R.S. Thomas stored in the BBC Wales studios in Cardiff. It was a fascinating experience for me to spend many hours watching him confidently arguing his strong views about Wales, the Welsh people, life and God.

'Mind your own business and be careful with foreigners' were my late mother's last words to me as I left Baghdad. My good fortune brought me to these shores, and Welsh poetry has been my biggest inspiration.

Introduction

John Barnie

Although they were born within eighteen months of each other, it is easy to think of R.S. Thomas and Dylan Thomas as belonging to different poetic generations. The younger of the two, Dylan, made his reputation in the 1930s with *18 Poems* (1934), *Twenty-Five Poems* (1936) and *The Map of Love* (1939); by 1953 he was dead.

By contrast, R.S. Thomas burned on a slower fuse. His debut collection, *The Stones of the Field* did not appear until 1946 and was followed by two locally produced pamphlets, *An Acre of Land* (1952) and *The Minister* (1953). It was not until the London publisher Rupert Hart-Davis brought out *Song at the Year's Turning* (1955) that R.S. Thomas came to the attention of a wider reading public. Over the next forty years, however, he produced a steady stream of collections that established his reputation as one of the finest English-language poets of the post-war years.

There are other differences between the two. Dylan Thomas was, foremost, a poet of south and west Wales who also moved in bohemian circles in London. R.S. was a poet of the isolated hill communities of mid Wales and of the sea and cliffs of Pen Llŷn. He became fluent in Welsh and wrote important autobiographical works in that language; and although he was by temperament a loner, he was politically engaged, with the peace movement and CND, but above all with the Welsh language movement of the 1960s and '70s, becoming a founder-member of Cyfeillion Llŷn (The Friends of Llŷn). It can almost be said that R.S. Thomas was a Welsh-language poet – in sensibility, at least – even though he wrote predominantly in English. It explains, I think, the interest in the man and his work in Welsh-language literary and cultural circles which no other English-language Welsh poet has achieved.

By vocation he was a priest in the Church in Wales. This brought him into contact – and sometimes into collision – with a wide range of people; it also, of course, underlies the great religious poetry of his late period. Yet he had a second vocation as an extremely knowledgeable amateur ornithologist, a vocation which took him out into the hills and woods and along the coast of Wales, and as far afield as Spain and Poland. These were times, perhaps, when he was most at ease with himself and the world.

When you follow a poet, collecting and reading his or her volumes as they appear, that writer becomes a part of your life, of your own intellectual and emotional being. When the poet dies the relationship changes, to be replaced by another which involves a re-evaluation; a reliving, too, of poems that are grounded in your own past and your own present. In this you share an experience and a sympathy with others among contemporaries who have followed the poet's career in the same way.

The span of human life is short, however. R.S. Thomas died in 2000; it will not be so long before those who knew him and who read his work in this way will also be no more. In this collection of centenary essays, therefore, leading writers, artists and cultural figures recall the poet they knew personally or the ways in which they engaged with R.S.'s poetry when they themselves were young, aspiring writers.

M. Wynn Thomas looks at Sarn Rhiw, the cottage to which the poet retired in 1978 which, he argues, played a major role in the great burst of creativity in his last decades. Barry Morgan, Archbishop of Wales, examines the contradictions that famously ran through the man and his work, while Gillian Clarke recalls a visit R.S. paid to her house in Cardiff which reveals a playful side that counters the austere view he often presented to the outside world. Jon Gower, himself an ardent birdwatcher, remembers a chance meeting with him while stranded by bad weather, waiting for the boat to Ynys Enlli. That encounter and Thomas's generosity to him, led to a friendship based on a mutual passion for birds. Artist Osi Rhys Osmond, by contrast, considers the bird as a metaphor for R.S. himself and recalls the CND campaigner he marched with, an aspect of the poet also discussed by Menna Elfyn; while bookseller and book collector Jeff Towns discusses covers and rare magazines in his extensive collection, relishing the hunt for the obscure and the hard to find.

Other contributors – Fflur Dafydd, Grahame Davies, Gwyneth Lewis – reveal the profound influence of R.S. Thomas on a much younger generation of poets, as does Peter Finch, who, it might be said, retained Thomas as a sort of touchstone for his own very different experimental work.

When a writer publishes a book, he or she never knows what effect it might have on others; it is launched on the world like a flock of doves over which he has relinquished control. These memoir-essays are testimonials to the variety of ways in which R.S. Thomas influenced profoundly the imaginations of readers during his lifetime. It is an engagement which will continue as new generations discover the poems for themselves – though not in the same way.

R.S. Thomas – Image and Reality

Barry Morgan

Most Press photographs of R.S. Thomas make him appear as wild, dour and unapproachable. The most recent volume, *Serial Obsessive*[1] by Professor M. Wynn Thomas, the poet's literary executor, has, on its front cover, the poet standing alone, looking out into the middle distance, hair blowing in the wind and an overcoat untidily belted. He looks incredibly austere.

The descriptions of him by many people have tended to match the photographic images – no bon vivant, cantankerous, misanthropic, curmudgeonly – a Welsh ogre. Allan Massie, the literary critic, compares him unfavourably to his contemporary, Dylan Thomas, who frequented the pubs of Soho and Fitzrovia, something he could not imagine R.S. Thomas doing. Indeed, in Richard Burton's recently published diaries,[2] the actor is scathing about the poet: 'I think the last tight smile that he allowed to grimace his features was at the age of 6 when he realised with delight that death was inevitable. He has consigned his wife to hell for a long time. She will recognise it when she goes there.'

Kyffin Williams sketched a line drawing of R.S. after his retirement. 'Look at it,' said R.S. to me once, 'It makes me look very miserable.' My reply gave him little consolation since I said he appeared so at times. All I got by way of a reply was 'Humph'.

Is that, however, a true reflection of the man? No one, of course, can truly know another human being and none of us are one dimensionable either. We are all complex people in the end and display different aspects of our personalities to different people at different times, depending on the occasion and what is happening in our lives. While not denying that some of these descriptions of R.S. contain truth, there were other aspects to his character and personality as well, and these different and varied sides are also reflected in his poetry.

I first met him when his first wife Elsi had just died and I went to offer my condolences. I had long been an admirer of his poetry but had never met him. After fighting my way through a pathway of bushes and brambles, I got to the door, which had written on it in chalk 'Cartref – R S Thomas' (R.S. Thomas's home). When I knocked, only the top half ·opened and he appeared, unsmiling and unwelcoming. I explained that I was the Archdeacon of Meirionnydd and had come to offer my condolences. His response was not the usual response of the bereaved. He told me that he had spent a lifetime avoiding people in the church hierarchy but since I had come, I'd better come in. He spent the next hour being absolutely charming and made me tea. We got on well after that first encounter. He wrote to me when I was elected Bishop of Llandaff in 1999 – I still have the letter – 'I do not congratulate you. I commiserate with you on your demotion.' He, of course, had hated living in Llandaff as a theological student.

This same quixotic mixture ran through his life. Visitors to the Llŷn would get short shrift if they spoke to him in English, when he pretended not to know the language or to be deaf. He railed against the Anglicisation of the Welsh countryside, seemed to acquiesce in the burning of holiday cottages, which in his view compounded the loss of the Welsh language since they were usually owned by English people, and was contemptuous of the people of Llŷn who earned their living from the tourist industry. I once witnessed him ask the Chairman at a public meeting in Pwllheli, when the lecture, as all the publicity had made clear, was going to be in English, in what language the obviously monoglot English lecturer was going to address the audience? On being told, he protested loudly, stood up and walked out from his seat in the front row, making a dramatic exit.

Yet his parishioners in Aberdaron still speak of his immense kindness in ministering to them, especially when people were old and dying, staying for hours at their bedside, although one of them did tell me that he thought that R.S. knew the species of birds in his parish better than the names of his parishioners. He would give people lifts in his car to the hospital in Bangor to visit their relatives, some sixty miles away, since they could get there no other way. He would teach the youngsters to play cricket in the garden of his vicarage and he was immensely kind to all manner of students researching his poetry, making himself available to them, even when they turned up on his door step unannounced. When a young man failed to produce his certificate of banns on his wedding morning, without which strictly speaking he could not be married, R.S. instead of turning him away, made enquiries of his friends and relatives whether they were willing to vouch for the fact that the banns had indeed been called. When assured that they had, although there was no written proof, he conducted the wedding so as not to spoil the day. The result for him was having to explain himself to a diocesan court called by his bishop and having to appear before the Diocesan Chancellor, who reprimanded him.

John G. McEllhenney, an American Episcopalian priest, has written a book entitled *A Masterwork of Doubting Belief.* In it are glimpses of the same quixotic nature of R.S. – in turn solicitous and kind, at other times almost offhand and rude. McEllhenney got to know him on his visits to Wales. When he wrote to him to say that he had booked a room at a guest house not far from Rhiw and gave him the address, R.S. said, 'It was no doubt run by English people who were happy to be part of the UK, the English concocted union of England, Wales and Scotland'. When McEllhenney wrote again for a suggestion about a Welsh-owned guest house instead of the one he had booked, R.S. replied, 'Best to stick with the English-owned guest house. Centuries of being subjected to English domination had bred a serf mentality in Welsh men and women who prefer to skivvy for the English than to risk running things themselves'.[3] McEllhenny says of him: 'To the world at large, Thomas was a stone faced crank, a recluse, a man who responded in Welsh to impertinent English questions. The man I learnt to know could break into a smile, enjoy table talk, savour ice-cream, and exhibited impish wit.'[4]

Thus, on another visit to Wales, Thomas took McEllhenney to the George III pub on the Mawddach Estuary in Penmaenpool, where they had a pint of bitter, steak and kidney pie and chips. McEllhenney reflects: 'Lunch with a Welshman who spoke highly refined English, at a pub named after an English monarch, on a river with a Welsh name, eating quintessential English pub grub.'[5] So too, on that same visit, when Thomas and McEllhenney and his friends were staying at separate guest houses in Aberdovey, and had arranged to meet at McEllhenney's guest house at 7.45pm, Thomas failed to arrive until 8.15pm. He said that he had been waiting for a call from their 'English inn-keeper'. The latter, however, told McEllhenney that she had rung Thomas shortly after McEllhenney had arrived that afternoon and told R.S. that he was expected for dinner at 7.45pm. There is also something quite ironic in an ardent Welshman willing to entertain and act as tour guide of north Wales to a group of Americans.

There is little doubt that he and his first wife lived ascetically. He himself implied that they silently moved around one another. The vicarage in Aberdaron was certainly cold and when they retired to a cottage in Rhiw, he ripped out the central heating because of the noise it made. He once ordered a vacuum cleaner and never used it again because of its noisiness. He confessed, in an interview with Graham Turner in *The Daily Telegraph*, 'I don't think I am a very loving person. I wasn't brought up in a loving home – my mother was afraid of emotion and you tend to carry on in the same way, don't you'.[6] Gwydion, his son, once said that the first double bed he saw was when he left home and that he never saw his parents touch one another. He said his father was austere and self contained and yet full of love he was unable to express except through his poems about Elsi:

> *One who was beautiful and grave and kind*
> *Who struck no discord in my dreaming mind...*[7]

> *Come to me a moment, stand,*
> *Ageing yet lovely, still...*[8]

In another poem written probably in the 1980s, he writes:

> *My luminary,*
> *my morning and evening*
> *star. My light at noon*
> *when there is no sun.*[9]

Yet his second marriage to Betty Thomas brought out the latent love within him. He had admitted in a poem about his father, 'all my life / I tried to keep love from bursting / its banks'.[10] It certainly did so when he married Betty. He doted on her and pandered to her wishes and enjoyed the world she opened up to him of cruises, holidays and meals in hotels, especially the Portmeirion in Porthmadog. He wrote to Mrs McEllhenney after being entertained by her and her husband on Ynys Môn: 'It is always fun to have a meal out'.[11] I once found R.S. and Betty outside Woolworth's in Bangor, trying to select a Christmas tree. I cannot imagine him doing that before his second marriage.

I once attended a party he gave in Llanfairynghornwy where he and Betty first lived after their marriage, where the wine and gin flowed freely and where the only Welsh speakers were R.S., my wife and myself, a retired professor and his wife, and the then leader of Plaid Cymru, Dafydd Wigley and his wife. All the others were either English visitors or local non Welsh-speaking gentry and R.S. appeared to be in his element.

Wynn Thomas, in his book *A Serial Obsessive*, quoting an interview of R.S.'s son Gwydion with Walford Davies says that 'During the years leading up to his second marriage to Betty Vernon, he moved to be near her in Titley, Herefordshire and was able to indulge his hankering to be an English country gentleman. He was to appear regularly in tweed jackets and cavalry twills like a retired colonel'.[12] He had, of course despised retired army officers when he was vicar of Eglwys-fach as some poems demonstrate:

> *And this one with his starched lip,*
> *his medals, his meanness;*
> *his ability to live cheap off dear things.*[13]

An ardent Welshman, he desperately wanted to write his poetry in Welsh, yet neither of his wives spoke Welsh and he sent his only son, Gwydion, to an English public school. In the most recent volume of poems gathered together posthumously, there is, however, a poem written in Welsh by him, 'Y Gwladwr'[14] and one is left wondering why he did not compose more.

His complex character is also evident in his attitude to the church. He once said that if anyone wanted to be a bishop, there was something wrong with his head and that 'the Church in Wales is run by a committee and most of what it does is fiddle faddle and he owed it nothing'.[15]

Yet, at other times, he said how grateful he was to that church for giving him time and space to write poetry and leisure to think and meditate while paying him a stipend. His pattern of life was to read and write in the morning, walk in the afternoon and visit parishioners in the evening. No other job would have enabled him to do that. He had retired when I became Bishop of Bangor, but I would think he could be a difficult priest to have in any diocese. I suspect he would not have attended Chapter meetings or diocesan events and would sit lightly to church structures. His bishop, as already indicated, took him to a diocesan court, probably because he was frustrated with him for other reasons. The Church in Wales did not seem to recognise his gifts as a poet. When I asked him in retirement to read his poetry in Bangor Cathedral when I had become the bishop, he protested that he was far too old and would not come. 'Leave him to me,' said Betty 'he will be there', and come he did, to a packed cathedral with hundreds of students, whose books he signed as if he had been doing so all his life. He was the life and soul of the party afterwards at Tŷ'r Esgob and Betty said that it had been a healing experience for him, as if after all these years, he had been acknowledged. He once read some of his poems at Great St Mary's Cambridge and met the then Bishop of Ely, Peter Walker, at supper afterwards. The latter loved poetry but when he asked R.S. the meaning of a particular poem, all he got by way of a reply was 'It is as it reads'. When the bishop persisted, saying, 'it can mean a whole host of things', R.S. replied, 'The poem is the poem.' 'So no explanation then?' said the bishop. 'Certainly not from me,' replied RS.

R.S.'s faith was an anguished one. Although he firmly believed in God, he refused to avoid in his poetry any of the hard questions such a belief entails. He questioned the nature of God in a world full of cruelty and chance and found it difficult to cope with God's seeming absence and hiddenness. Prayer was a particular problem since God seemed never to answer it:

Yes, I know what he is like:
a kind of impossible robot
you insert your prayers into
like tickets, that after a while
are returned, to you with the words
'Not granted' written upon them.[16]

Yet he combined this liberal theology with extreme conservatism as far as the liturgy of the church was concerned. He refused to celebrate the Eucharist facing the congregation, preferring to lead with his back to it and facing the Almighty, as he put it. He disliked modern liturgy and modern versions of the Bible since he believed they had lost a sense of the numinous. He had been influenced by St Michael's College more than he realised.

He was a mass of contradictions and inconsistencies in all kinds of ways. He frequently wrote about a God who could not be pinned down, was ultimately unknowable and unfathomable. God could not be described except through metaphor and symbol. He himself seemed to delight in the same characteristics.

He was partly misunderstood because he had a mischievous dry sense of humour. He liked teasing people and he did so in such a deadpan way that one was never sure whether one was being teased or not. He said that in his poetry, he was often ironic and people did not realise that and the same was true of his encounters with people.

R.S. used to say that he preferred solitude and nature to people and indeed in some of his poems about the farmers of Manafon he seems to despise them:

Dreams clustering thick on his sallow skull,
Dark as curls, he comes, ambling with his cattle
From the starved pastures.[17]

Motionless, except when he leans to gob in the fire.
There is something frightening in the vacancy of his mind.[18]

Yet, in another poem, he writes:

> *Don't be taken in*
> *By stinking garments or aimless grin;*
> *He also is human, and the same small star,*
> *That lights you homeward, has inflamed his mind*
>
> *With the old hunger, born of its kind.*[19]

Here again is a mixture of seeming contempt and yet tenderness for his parishioners. Towards the end of his life, he told me that he had been too harsh in his strictures on farmers and that they had been nothing but kind to him and his family. He felt that he had also been too harsh on his mother.

The same complexity of character is seen in Thomas's religious poetry. He admitted that he found it difficult to be an 'orthodox believer and that Christian beliefs were an attempt to convey through language something that is unsayable'.[20] Thus he writes poetry where he seems to believe little:

> *And in the book I read :*
> *God is love. But lifting*
> *my head, I do not find it*
> *so.*[21]

So too:

> *I never thought other than,*
> *That God is that great absence*
> *In our lives, the empty silence*
> *Within, the place where we go*
> *Seeking, not in hope to*
> *Arrive or find.*[22]

Yet he can also write of God:

Many creatures
reflect you, the flowers
your colour, the tides, the precision
of your calculations.[23]

And for him, God's darkness implied his presence for

It is not your light that
can blind us; it is the splendour
of your darkness.[24]

He was not a systematic theologian but someone who reflected both his doubts and his faith in his poetry, so that on a superficial level it seemed as if he believed little. Yet God was never far away from his thoughts and he believed that pursuing a relationship with him was the most worthwhile thing anyone could do. For him, God's hiddenness did not preclude being able to find him and it is obvious from his poetry and the way he prayed, that he spent many hours in church 'waiting for the God to speak'.[25]

He searched and longed for God and for him the question was not whether God existed but the kind of God he is. For him, God was revealed supremely in and through the person of Jesus for he is 'Love's risen body'.[26]

He says, in spite of all his doubts and questions:

You have answered
us with the image of yourself
on a hewn tree, suffering
injustice, pardoning it.[27]

The poet and his poetry seem all of a piece not always easy or easy to understand and his questioning mind raised fundamental questions about God, evil, prayer and Jesus. Yet the paradox is that through his willingness to be so honest and open he has helped many people in their own faith journeys.

Notes

1: M. Wynn Thomas, *Serial Obsessive* (University of Wales Press: Cardiff, 2013).

2: *The Richard Burton Diaries*, ed. Chris Williams (Yale University Press: New Haven, 2012).

3: John G. McEllhenney, *A Masterwork of Doubting-Belief: R.S. Thomas and his Poetry* (Wipf and Stock: Eugene, Oregon, 2013), p. 4.

4: *A Masterwork of Doubting-Belief*, p. 12.

5: *A Masterwork of Doubting-Belief*, p. 50.

6: Quoted by Wynn Thomas, *Serial Obsessive*, p. 3.

7: 'I never thought', c. 1939 in *R.S. Thomas, Uncollected Poems*, ed. Tony Brown and Jason Walford Davies (Bloodaxe Books: Tarset, 2013).

8: 'Birthday', *Uncollected Poems*.

9: 'Luminary', *Uncollected Poems*.

10: 'The Father Dies', *Uncollected Poems*.

11: *A Masterwork of Doubting-Belief*, p. 7.

12: *Serial Obsessive*, p. 65.

13: *The Echoes Return Slow* (Macmillan: London, 1988), p. 52.

14: *Uncollected Poems*.

15: *A Masterwork of Doubting-Belief*, p. 53.

16: 'Ivan Karamazov', *Collected Poems, 1945-1990* (Phoenix Books: London, 1993).

17: 'Out of the Hills', *Collected Poems*.

18: 'A Peasant', *Collected Poems*.

19: 'Affinity', *Collected Poems*.

20: *David Jones Journal* (2001), p. 93-102.

21: 'Which', *Collected Poems*.

22: 'Via Negativa', *Collected Poems*.

23: 'Alive', *Collected Poems*.

24: 'Shadows', *Collected Poems*.

25: 'Kneeling', *Collected Poems*.

26: 'The Answer', *Collected Poems*.

27: 'Tell Us', *Mass for Hard Times* (Bloodaxe Books: Tarset, 1992), p. 46.

Wrestling with Ronald: R.S. Thomas at 100

Gwyneth Lewis

We only quarrel with people who are important to us and make up with those who are essential. In school in the 1970s we were forced to read poems from R.S. Thomas's most strident nationalist phase, including the assertion that we were incestuous and terminally backward-looking. Oh, great. As a national self-image, this didn't chime with the critical verve I felt about the culture I'd inherited. It smelt of self-flagellation so, exams done, I thought there'd be no more R.S. Thomas for me.

In the 1980s I decided that I wanted to be a poet and began to read my Welsh predecessors seriously, to see what was left for me to do. There was a shock waiting for me in Thomas's prose. In 1943, heavily influenced by Patrick Kavanagh, Thomas had published 'A Peasant', his first description of Iago Prytherch as a vacant yob spitting into the hearth. In an essay 'The Depopulation of the Welsh Hill Country'[1] published two years later, Thomas describes hill farmers as merry as birds. *Happy*? What happened to primeval misery? I felt that I'd caught R.S. out in a lie. To my mind, nationalism based on rigged evidence or a poet's preferred tone of voice on any given day was bogus. So, for a second time, I thought I'd wipe my hands of his work. What I hadn't understood then was that Thomas's Wales was always a fiction, his name for an ideal – if debased – spiritual condition.

By then, I'd already met R.S. and liked him. He'd been invited to give a reading at the Cambridge Union, and he agreed to let me interview him for a student magazine. Not only was Thomas a stern figure, with his long, lean face, his calling as a vicar made him an even more forbidding prospect. I was so frightened of him that I wouldn't go without a friend. Against all expectation, R.S. was charming and we stayed the whole afternoon. At his reading, he was asked if he thought that Dante was the imagination of Christendom. 'No,' he replied, 'Christ is the imagination of Christendom.' I'd just stopped being religious but this statement rang me like a bell. It's the single most useful and mysterious statement about poetry I've ever heard.

It was ten years before we met again and we fell immediately into the kind of teasing bicker we'd established at our first meeting. By the end of his life, we were good friends. I realise that this assessment of R.S. Thomas's work has started out more like an attack than an appreciation. This is because the aesthetic and moral choices that R.S. Thomas made matter to me. Love isn't gauged by uncritical positive regard: any true account of one's heritage needs to include disagreements and disappointments, as well as admiration.

The discrepancy between R.S.'s public persona – which was austere – and his private company (playful, funny and delightful) has drawn much comment. I've often wondered about what effect the exclusion of lighter aspects of his personality from his writing had meant for his achievement. R.S. was a compelling reader but the cumulative effect could be grim. After one recital at the Hay Festival, I offered to kill my companion before committing suicide myself. Yet, there are many comic touches in the poems, my favourite being in *The Minister*, a short play, where he describes the moonlight's bottom pressing against the manse's window pane. This side of R.S. was largely, but not entirely, suppressed, in later work. Was this tone – which I've already identified in his poetic politics – also the result of emotional willfulness? If so, was I right in thinking it a liability?

In 1963 Thomas edited *The Penguin Book of Religious Verse*, which reads like a sourcebook of his own writing. This surprising volume shows that R.S. was a voracious and heterodox reader. Byron appears several times, with Tennyson, Swinburne, Browning, Herrick, Campion, Robinson Jeffers and many others. M. Wynn Thomas told me only recently that R.S. spoke French and read a good deal in that language. As he matured as a poet, Thomas dropped his obsession with the Condition of Wales and undertook a serious exploration of particle physics. This was a progressive and unusual subject for poetry in 1979. Many of these poems named the Machine as an enemy of man. This category led to confusion for many readers who thought Thomas anti-science. In an interview with John Barnie, Thomas reflected that science and religion were not necessarily incompatible; it was the pursuit of technology in the name of profit that was the problem. If science is a means of probing reality, he suggested, its difference from religion was essentially one of method.[2]

The Machine, therefore, also represents, as Daniel Westover puts it, 'rote, (often dangerously) non-judicious thinking.'[3] You could say that R.S. himself was leaving the Machine of his own wishful politics and developing as a free-verse pioneer of major themes such as eco-theology, at the forefront of the most acute modern dilemmas.

R.S. once recommended a poem called 'Black Marigolds' 'translated' from the Sanskrit by E. Powys Mathers. I found it in an Anvil edition with a foreword by Tony Harrison. It wasn't what I'd expected of a vicar:

> *Even now*
> *The pleasèd intimacy of rough love*
> *Upon the patient glory of her form*
> *Racks me with memory; and her bright dress*
> *As it were yellow flame, which the white hand*
> *Shamefastly gathers in her rising haste,*
> *The slender grace of her departing feet.*[4]

Mathers used Eastern poetry and Pessoan personae to explore alcoholism, drug addiction and bisexuality. And yet, R.S. became a great love poet himself. Having been publishing since the 1940s, he wrote his best work in his late seventies and eighties. For example, the poem 'No Time' from his last collection, *No Truce with the Furies*, published in 1995, pairs his observation of birds with the loss of his first wife. The lyric invokes those other great poems of widowhood, Thomas Hardy's work of 1912-13.

The skill in R.S. Thomas's prosody has been consistently underestimated. Because his vocabulary is plain, critics have only recently begun to describe the metrical argument in the movement of his lines, aside from his explicit subject matter. R.S. told me once that he had aspired to write like Wallace Stevens. I asked him how he decided what should be his third line, given that he wasn't using fixed stanzas. 'Put two lines together and let them breed' was his disingenuous answer. I recently found the exact same word used in one of Dylan Thomas's letters. This could be coincidence, but it's a suggestive one. Dylan's modernist surrealism and R.S.'s seemingly direct spiritual autobiography may have more in common than previously thought. In his recent masterful account of various contexts in which Thomas worked, M. Wynn Thomas has drawn attention to him as a serious reader of American poetry.[5] Thomas the priest modeled his free verse on the work of William Carlos Williams, and read Sylvia Plath, Denise Levertov and others carefully. *The Echoes Return Slow* first published in 1988 is considered by critics to be Thomas's most avant-garde volume for its mixture of prose and poetry.

Much of Thomas's best work plays units of the eye against units of sound.[6] Thomas's poems are often so slim on the page that the eye is able to take them in at one glance, spot-reading key words out of their explicit order. The ear can't do this, so we are given two perceptions of the poem: a magnetic and true reading. Thomas makes the uncertainty principle of enjambement, his great tool, unsettle our normal assumptions. This is the sign of a great poet, one who plays two tunes on the one line. Now that Thomas's *Uncollected Poems* have been edited by Tony Brown and Jason Walford Davies, what we need is a complete critical edition.

Although R.S. Thomas was nominated for the Nobel in Literature, it was always unlikely that he was going to win it. His poetry was certainly of a high enough calibre but he was never plugged in firmly enough to the literary world to give him the reputational momentum that can result in a phone call from Sweden. He told me many times that he disagreed with the whole idea of competition in literature, a sobering thought for a Welsh-speaker like me, who cut my teeth on writing poems on set subjects for prizes. I assumed that this was to do with his conception of writing poetry as a spiritual discipline. We were once together on the short list for the Arts Council of Wales's Book of the Year Prize, against Nigel Jenkins's *Gwalia in Khasia*. The winner was due to receive £3,000 and the runners-up £1,000 each. Before the evening, we decided to work together. R.S. said that I could have the glory if he could have the money. I objected because I needed the money as well. So we agreed that, if one of us came first and we combined our winnings we could both take home £2,000 apiece. It was a fine plan but Nigel Jenkins, the sod, was awarded the prize and R.S. and I ended up short on both cash and prestige.

R.S. was slow to praise. He took a pretty dim view of some lionised contemporary poets but also dismissed his own writing as 'old hat'. This statement combined humility with a certain kind of assurance, suggesting that it was only the literary world's perception that made him seem so, rather than his work itself. The hat might be old but it was still a hat to be considered. The letters that I received from R.S. are now in the National Library of Wales. He would answer by return of post and in a bracingly direct manner – no filler pleasantries or flourishes. I'm deeply grateful to have known him and to have been allowed to glimpse some of the choices a great poet had made in his life and also to feel what those decisions had cost him. It's part of the package and poets rarely speak of it.

Notes

1: *R.S. Thomas: Selected Prose*, ed. Sandra Anstey (Poetry Wales Press: Bridgend, 1983), p. 21.

2: Quoted in Daniel Westover, *R.S. Thomas: A Stylistic Biography* (University of Wales Press: Cardiff, 2011), p. 132.

3: Ibid.

4: E. Powys Mathers, *Black Marigold and Coloured Stars* (Anvil Press: London, 2004), p. 91.

5: M. Wynn Thomas, *R.S. Thomas: Serial Obsessive* (University of Wales Press: Cardiff, 2013), pp. 241-62.

6: See Westover, pp. 152-69.

A version of this essay first appeared in *Poetry Review*.

The Poet of Sarn Rhiw

M. Wynn Thomas

Cwestiwn: pryd mae bwthyn yn debyg i dŵr? Ateb: pan fydd y bwthyn yn Sarn Rhiw.

Dyna un enw ar y bwthyn bach di-nod o gyfnod y brenin Iago a ddaeth yn gartref i R.S. Thomas yn ei flynyddoedd olaf, ar ôl iddo ymddeol fel ficer Aberdaron. Ac yn y llecyn hudolus hwn y cynhyrchodd ran helaeth o'r swmp o waith y seilir ei amlygrwydd fel un o feirdd crefyddol mwyaf yr ugeinfed ganrif arno.

Naddwyd Sarn y Plas (i roi iddo ei enw arall) o feini hynafol penrhyn Llŷn, ac y mae'r hen fwthyn yn cysgodi'n dwt yng nghesail y llethrau uwchben Porth Neigwl, bae twyllodrus y drylliwyd aml i long hwylio ynddo slawer dydd, a mynd yn ysglyfaeth i'r llong-ddryllwyr barus lleol.

Question: when is a cottage like a tower? Answer: when the cottage in question is Sarn Rhiw.

Otherwise known as Sarn y Plas, this small, humble Jacobean cottage was where R.S. Thomas spent most of his final years following his retirement as vicar of Aberdaron in 1978. And it was in this atmospheric location that he produced most of the memorable body of work that heralded his emergence as one of the great religious poets of modern times.

Built, or rather quarried, from the ancient boulders of the Llŷn peninsula (the long, west-pointing arm of north Wales), the low-lying cottage cleaves to the contours of its landscape. It nestles self-protectively into a gentle, but exposed, slope above the dramatic shingle of Porth Neigwl, a bay whose shallows used to prove so treacherous in the days of sailing ships that the locals in this isolated spot acquired a reputation for being excellent wreckers.

I first visited R.S. there with a companion in the late eighties. We were very kindly received not only by him but by his shy, self-effacing but sharply alert wife, Elsi, who served us home-made cakes and jam. 'You don't speak Welsh?' my companion remarked to the retiring Mrs Thomas. 'I did try,' came the quiet reply: 'I even attended some classes, but the first time I came home and tried a phrase on Ronald, he snorted "Huh, you speak Welsh like a South Walian." And I never tried again.'

The Welsh language: a few years after settling in Sarn Rhiw, R.S. celebrated his cottage in a poem hinging on a proud, intense affirmation that he now lived in a house whose very materials seemed to speak the language of its physical and cultural location. For much of his adult life, the fate of Welsh had been one of the most consistent, and most fraught, of the poet's concerns. His final move, as priest in the Church in Wales, to the Llŷn peninsula, had been largely predicated on the assumption that there, at last, he could be part of a Welsh-speaking community that was settled, rooted, and culturally committed. But once more, his life's dream was fated to be significantly – if not completely – disappointed. He found a community seasonally invaded by English-speaking tourists and already fatally corrupted – at least according to his own exacting standards – by a craven eagerness to pander to the visitors' tastes. In the relative isolation of his retirement, his disappointment found constructive expression in wholehearted practical involvement in the damage-limitation work of Cyfeillion Llŷn (The Friends of Llŷn) and other cognate campaign groups. But alongside bold, outspoken and controversial public action there also ran a loner's impulse to retreat to private strength.

Throughout his career, R.S. Thomas had resorted, when under this kind of intense cultural pressure, to a rather desperate elementalising of the beleaguered Welsh language, as had become strikingly evident in his poem 'Welcome' which warned the visitor that while (s)he might enter Wales physically with the utmost ease the essence of the country would remain inaccessible to all save those who learnt the language. For him, the massive boulders of Sarn Rhiw likewise became psychically reassuring guarantors of the long-term survival of the language of its early seventeenth-century builders. And in thus associating his cottage with the survival of his beloved culture, he may well have been recollecting the twentieth-century poet Waldo Williams's celebrated lines defining what it meant to value national identity. 'Beth yw gwladgarwch?' (What is patriotism?), Waldo enquired, before famously replying that it meant 'Cadw tŷ / Mewn cwmwl tystion' (Keeping house / In a cloud of witnesses).[1]

Thomas was deeply aware of keeping house in such a mystic company at Sarn Rhiw. He felt himself to be answerable to these companionable but exacting ghosts and wondered whether he would eventually be judged to have been equal to their implicit challenge. Would Sarn Rhiw (and therefore the language and culture that for him were preserved in its very stones) one day grant him the privilege of being counted amongst its guardian ghosts, he wondered.

The cottage's garden provided Thomas with what was, for him, the perfect distant, selective outlook on the rest of Wales that he otherwise viewed with such deep suspicion and distaste. He could see the peak of Cadair Idris from his study window, and in fine weather the garden afforded him views of Snowdon (Wales's highest mountain), Cadair Idris and other eminences such as Y Cnicht, Y Moelwynion and Y Rhinogau. This is R.S.'s version of a romantic Wild Wales, the psycho-geography of his creative imagination.

It is becoming evident, then, that for R.S. Thomas 'Sarn Rhiw' was much more than an old cottage. As Gaston Bachelard resonantly suggested in *The Poetics of Space*, poetry offers us abundant evidence that dwellings have the habit of inhabiting our imaginations, of becoming 'the topography of our intimate being.'[2] And it is by bearing this in mind that we may come to see how much Thomas's cottage resembles a famous tower. The tower in question is that of his favourite poet, W.B. Yeats, through the magic medium of whose poetry the semi-derelict Norman tower he bought in Gort, in the far west of Ireland, and painstakingly restored was turned into a remarkable storehouse of emblems seminal to his extraordinary imaginative existence. For him, Thoor Ballylee, a multi-storied tower with a winding stair, represented the spirit's ascent to exalted, esoteric knowledge, while in the stubborn persistence of its massive stone walls Yeats discerned signs of the stubborn endurance throughout the centuries of the superior, aristocratic Anglo-Norman cultural tradition of Ireland with which he was so anxious to associate his own family pedigree. Yeats thus turned his tower into the primary enabling myth of his mature poetry, and R.S. Thomas likewise turned Sarn Rhiw into one of the primary enabling myths of his own late, great period of spiritual search.

For him, his cultural, spiritual and environmental concerns all seemed to converge and cohere at Sarn y Plas. Several years after I had first met him there, I had another opportunity to visit, this time in the company of a film crew intent on preparing an ambitious documentary portrait of the aged poet. I remember him good-naturedly complying with the request that he sit at a desk pretending to write – a clichéd image of the poet at work, as he very well knew. And as he did so he chuckled as he imagined naively impressed viewers exclaiming, 'Look, he's a real poet after all. Who knows, he might even have been able to win the crown at the National Eisteddfod!'[3]

Towards the end of a full day's filming, he took me on a walk along the lane high above Porth Neigwl and, as we chatted, I took the opportunity to pick up a stone that now sits on my desk as a memento of the place and of the occasion, and as a memorial to the man. I chose it because it seemed an apt emblem of his special relationship to the rocky landscape out of which his cottage had been virtually carved. In an extended passage in his autobiography *Neb* (Nobody) that offers us the best insight into the complex of elements that constituted his myth of Sarn Rhiw, R.S. makes special mention of its dolerite surroundings. And how expressive of his own creative temperament it seems that his home should have been made of volcanic rock that had hardened as it cooled.

The providential nature of the cottage seems underlined by the fact that it was far from being the poet's chosen location. Following retirement, he would have preferred to stay on at Aberdaron rectory, and, failing that, he and his wife seriously considered accepting the Keating sisters' initial offer of a larger cottage in the vicinity. Moreover, the eventual decision to opt for Sarn Rhiw was a costly one for them both, since it involved sacrificing, in R.S. Thomas's case, a working library and, in his wife's case, the work area, wall-space, and light so crucial to her work as a talented artist.

But very much against the odds, the move to his home on a slope overlooking Porth Neigwl turned out to be profoundly auspicious. Here, he gradually grew to appreciate a home whose very stones seemed to be an index of the culture of the early builders. And, most importantly of all, he began to register the proximity of the sea, whose sound seemed not just to penetrate but to permeate the very stones of his cottage, so that he and it seemed to be co-habiting intimately.

A house, Bachelard observed, can serve humans as 'an instrument with which to confront the cosmos.' (*PS*, p. 46) 'A house that is as dynamic as this,' he writes elsewhere, 'allows the poet to inhabit the universe. Or, to put it differently, the universe comes to inhabit his house.' (*PS*, p. 51) It is for precisely this quality that R.S. came most to appreciate Sarn y Plas. It literally 'placed' him in a special relationship to nature, and indeed to the whole cosmos. Thus, in *Blwyddyn yn Llŷn* (A Year in Llŷn), his journal of the passage of the seasons on a peninsula numinous with spiritual implications, he recalls how on occasions the cottage seemed almost porous, as tiny bats (*Pipistrellus pipistrellus*) exercised their ancient right to zig-zag at twilight through the house. They entered, as they had done for four centuries, through the large central chimney.

And then there was light's miraculous penetration of the cottage's dark interiors. Every time R.S. saw its shaft strike a boulder that had for so long stood in place, he felt like a prisoner briefly released from the confines of his narrow cell. Most importantly of all, for the son of a sailor who had been raised in Holyhead and had the salt of the sea in his veins, the cottage resounded with the sea's moods. On one occasion, he raised his head from his desk just in time to catch sight of a gannet just before it hit the water. And at night, the stones seemed to register the shock of crashing waves that had begun their journey way out in the Atlantic. As a result, his late period is notable for its serial meditations on the great waters that, at Sarn Rhiw, constantly met his eyes and haunted his ears.

But if it was the sea that consumed his attention below the cottage, behind it lay a wood thronged with birds. Their cries and songs took him back in memory to the Holyhead childhood that had echoed to the raucous, raw calls of gulls. In this respect, too, Sarn Rhiw served him well. Here he could keep intimate company with the bird life that, as he confessed in *Blwyddyn yn Llŷn*, had long solaced him for the shortcomings of humanity at large, and of his inadequate compatriots in particular. And just as the neighbouring wood provided birds with shelter, Sarn Rhiw came for him to function partly as a sanctuary. It helped him realise, for one final, conclusive time, how much he owed to his wife, Elsi, and how deeply indebted he was to her quiet, self-effacing, cherishing and nurturing love. He accordingly paid moving homage to her quiet, supportive fidelity and constancy in a number of delicate, touching late poems. Even as he wrote them, he must have been painfully aware that the time remaining to them together was very short. Elsi passed away in 1991, and with her passing, Sarn Rhiw came, for R.S., to assume one final, and tragically sinister, complexion.

From the beginning, one of his images of the cottage had been that of a hermitage, with himself as hermit. After all, so small was it compared to the spacious vicarage he and his wife had occupied at Aberdaron, that they'd had to dispose of many of their cherished books and paintings in order to accommodate themselves to their straitened means. But in due course R.S. came to view even this act as providential – as facilitating that final stripping of oneself of the distracting accoutrements of life preparatory to facing one's end. And after his wife's death, he returned to this image with a haunting intensity in one of the most powerful of his late poems, turning his bare, tiny bedroom into a monk's cell suited to the complete devotion of himself to prayer.

The poem, however, proved to be little more than a desperate fantasy of solitary survival. R.S. may well have been a notorious loner, but he was not as much of a loner as many – possibly including himself – had supposed. The death of his wife hit him very hard, and in his loneliness and isolation he teetered, at times, on the very brink of delusion and breakdown. For fifteen years, Sarn Rhiw had served R.S. well as a fertile source of emblems that nurtured his imagination and sustained his psyche. But now, at the last, it failed him, turning from a sanctuary into an isolation cell, an asylum of the self. On one of the occasions I met with him during that desolate period of his life, he confessed that at times he was disturbed by his own reflection in the mirror, fearing he could detect there the ominous beginnings of the disintegration of his ego. Several of his late poems testify in anguished terms to his failure to escape the Furies that seemed to him intent on vengefully tracking his footsteps to the very end. He would, he now came to realise, never be able to resolve the dark enigma of his own identity. Old age would never bring him the benediction of belated wisdom. At the last, Sarn Rhiw therefore turned into nightmare, from which R.S. was eventually to be released only through his second marriage to Betty Vernon. But in the few years remaining to him he was never to recover that energy and penetration of imaginative vision that had been the gift of Sarn y Plas.

I first met Betty at the very end of that day's filming at Sarn Rhiw early in 1994. 'She's an old friend, kindly staying with me,' R.S. said as he somewhat awkwardly introduced her. There had been no inkling of her presence before she suddenly appeared, as if she'd materialised out of the stone. But Betty was no ghost, and it was impossible to imagine spirits lingering long in her vicinity. Voluble, extrovert and stylishly dressed, she was the antithesis of Elsi. Approaching eighty, she was still game for anything. 'Never leave the house without lipstick and make-up, my dear,' she once pityingly confided to my wife: 'You never know your luck.'

And it didn't take her long to winkle R.S. out of what had become his reluctant hermitage at Sarn Rhiw. Indeed, even before their relationship had become public knowledge, he had spent a winter in her company on the English border, a hundred long miles away from the cottage. A friend recently recalled how, as Thomas prepared to break the news to him that he would be moving away, the poet 'stared vaguely and dumbly out of the tiny window in the direction of Porth Neigwl.'[4] Over the coming years, R.S. would often intimate that he regretted the break with Sarn y Plas and mourned the loss of the sea. And another friend has likewise testified affectingly to his special bond with the place:

*How many times did I linger near Sarn Rhiw, that summer
after he had finally left Llŷn, and feel a lump of hiraeth?
Many a time. And to this day, I find it difficult to pass by
without pausing for a second. His influence is still to be felt
here, as it is throughout Wales too.* (CRS, p. 80)

For the first time since R.S. Thomas's passing, I visited the
characterful old cottage earlier this summer – or rather, I visited the
vicinity, because Sarn itself remains safely in the hands of the Thomas
family. I had just paid a visit to Oriel Plas Glyn-y-Weddw, where I had
much enjoyed a rare exhibition of the fastidious paintings of Elsi
Thomas, professionally known as Mildred Eldridge. As I'd wended my
way through the beautiful springtime landscape of Llŷn the clouds had
been hanging balefully low over the peninsula and a fine rain was in the
air. But then, just as I arrived at the cottage, the sky suddenly cleared,
and the whole breathtaking prospect below and before me was suffused
with light. It was as if I had stumbled miraculously upon R.S. Thomas's
famous bright field. It seemed that Sarn Rhiw had lived up to the
numinous reputation secured for it in the writings of Thomas's late prime.

But then came disappointment. Just beyond the cottage I found
myself stayed by an ominous notice: 'Road closed.' The way to Sarn y
Plas, I realised, now led only to a dead end. Ahead, the narrow cliff road
crumbled dangerously away. And a new road to the old substantial house
of Plas yn Rhiw had been pushed through behind and above the cottage.
What dire cultural omens and environmental metaphors, I ruefully
pondered, would Sarn y Plas's most famous inhabitant have morosely
discovered in such unsympathetic developments?

Notes

1: Waldo Williams, *Dail Pren* (Gomer: Llandysul, 1957), p. 67.

2: Gaston Bachelard, *The Poetics of Space,* trans. Maria Jolas (Beacon Press: Boston,
1994), p. xxxvi. Hereafter *PS*.

3: The National Eisteddfod is the very large, annual, multi-cultural Festival to celebrate
Welsh-language culture. The high points of the event are the awarding of a crown and
of a chair to the winners of the two main poetry competitions of the Eisteddfod.

4: *Cofio R.S.* (Gwasg y Bwthyn: Caernarfon, 2013), p. 48. Hereafter *CRS*.

The Girl Who Went into the East: A Student's Guide to R.S.

Fflur Dafydd

Although I can't recall the exact moment that my long-standing love affair with the poetry of R.S. Thomas began, I certainly remember the moment it dawned on me that his poetry meant more to me than the work of any other writer. It was 1995, and I was 16, sitting in a classroom in Ysgol Gyfun Dyffryn Teifi, completing the task set by our English teacher, which was to make a list of all our set texts in terms of preference. At first glance, it was a simple enough task. But then, when you considered the materials we had to choose from – Gerard Manley Hopkins, Tennessee Williams, Emily Brontë, Jane Austen – these were rich pickings. It is rather strange, looking back, that the name I scrawled down first, without hesitation, was R.S. Thomas. The set text was *Selected Poems: 1946-1968*, the Bloodaxe edition featuring a grimacing R.S. in his dog-collar – hardly the kind of image that would grab the attention of young, impressionable schoolgirls. And yet, even seeing that edition now brings back a surge of memories – not of the school, my class mates, or of my misspent youth – but of moments of discovery. Moments of awakening. I recall vividly reading the poem 'Concession' for the first time, and being moved to tears by it. I also remember *The Minister* taking deep root in me, enabling me to take my first, tentative steps into poetry, through drafting my own (terrible) long poem. Even though my life experience was extremely limited, R.S. Thomas was somehow able to pervade every aspect of it. In chapel on Sundays I found myself trying to analyse its silences, while on Saturdays, I waited on tables and dealt with rude tourists, thinking all the while of the 'small windows' being dirtied. So reluctant was I to let go of this wondrous poetry collection that, when it came to handing the books back at the end of the year, I asked the teacher if I could keep it. With joy, I heard another classmate make the same request. For a moment, I thought I had found a kindred spirit – until she explained to me that the reason she couldn't return it was because she'd written a list of all the boys she'd ever kissed on the front page.

Although I wasn't aware of it back then, R.S. had become the single most important writer I would ever read, whose works would inform the person, and the writer, I would become. Even something as rudimentary as my choice of degree was informed by him. I was a girl from the countryside who spoke only Welsh at home, who had a Welsh-language poet for a mother and a Welsh-language activist for a father, and whom everyone expected to go on to study Welsh at university. And yet I had already formed a deep attachment to the unfamiliar tongue that R.S. had presented to me with such tenderness. It contained such possibility, somehow, such *otherness*. Of course, it is only now I understand the irony of things: that the very tongue R.S. found so problematic, the language he would rather not have written in, according to him, was the one he'd made so appealing to me – a Welsh speaker, from a Welsh-speaking family who'd been given everything from birth that he'd desperately wanted. Going on to study English, at Aberystwyth? It didn't make sense to anyone but me at the time. But that decision, made all those years ago, was to lead me to R.S. Thomas's doorstep, quite literally. It would take me across the stone threshold of Sarn y Plas in Rhiw, albeit a decade too late.

I decided to write a dissertation on his poetry in my final year, and by this time I was discovering terms such as *post-colonial*, and latching on, as all undergraduates do, to a new theory with a wide-eyed wonder, thinking it somehow explained away Thomas's entire predicament. I soon made an application to study a Welsh Writing in English MA at Swansea. But the plan changed. Because by then, R.S. had awakened something else in me – the desire to become a writer.

I abandoned my academic self somewhere on the M4, and found myself travelling eastwards to take up a Creative Writing MA at East Anglia. There was a thrill in this, as well as an awakening. When I talked Welsh on my mobile phone around campus, some people assumed I was conversing in Arabic. The idea of a separate, non-British, Welsh identity was totally incomprehensible to the vast majority of the people I met in East Anglia, and there were times where this attitude deeply shocked me. When a friend came to stay we conversed in Welsh in the back of a taxi, and the taxi driver actually demanded that we spoke in English. We stormed out of the taxi in defiance, finding ourselves in the middle of a busy ring-road, in the rain, having gained nothing. It was an act that left us helpless, cold; having to walk extra miles to catch a train back home: which is, in fact, quite symptomatic of the predicament of the bilingual writer, who often has to travel much further than anyone else and still ends up nowhere in the end.

Despite this, I persisted with the English experience. East Anglia University was, and is, a vibrant, dynamic place to be, and it seemed that staying on in Norwich to take up yet another degree in Creative Writing, was the next step for me. I met with lecturers, I applied to start my PhD in Creative Writing there, day-dreaming of the day my first novel – in English – would be published. Until I saw a poster which changed everything. Always in life there are turning points, fateful beginnings which somehow seal your future – a moment that lets the future in, to paraphrase Grahame Greene. And this was it. The poster advertising the inaugural R.S. Thomas scholarship at Bangor University, hung askew on a pin-board in East Anglia's English Department, was a signpost. Away from the east, and westwards towards that wild garden of Sarn y Plas in Rhiw.

And that's when my story begins, in many ways, just as R.S. Thomas's story ends. Because as I was driving to Bangor University to meet my PhD supervisor, Professor Tony Brown, an announcement came on the radio that R.S. had died that very morning. The very day I entered into the possibility of meeting him, making him the subject of my life's work, he disappeared. There was something very 'Thomosian' about it, if I can coin that phrase. It was the room I entered from which someone had just gone. And yet perhaps things were meant to be this way. It was a moment, like many other moments, that bound us even closer together, though we had never met. It was an *uncanny* moment, in the Freudian sense, the uncanny being a theory I had not then discovered, but which would, later on, become my means of understanding R.S. and his many contradictions and complexities. 'The uncanny is that class of the frightening which leads back to what is known of old and long familiar', writes Freud, and indeed it is this strange conjunction of the familiar and the alien that is the dynamic of the uncanny's power to disturb, and the very reason I felt that R.S., caught between cultures and languages, seemed prey to certain moments of 'uncanniness' throughout his life. Now I, too, was haunted by our near-meeting, a deeply unsettling feeling which made my arrival in Bangor seem almost inappropriate, like being the first on the scene of a terrible tragedy, hoping to gain something from it.

But somehow, for me to find myself, as I embarked on my thesis, in this strange, liminal, uncanny place, felt almost fitting. Laying claim to him in an academic sense, insisting I would be able to 'get to know' R.S, just as the opportunity to 'know' him as a person had vanished, highlighted the absurdity of ever really knowing anyone, let alone a writer as complex as R.S. And far from being absent, he was now strikingly present – staring at me from obituaries, tributes, and memorials, making it harder to keep up with him than when he was alive. His death only seemed to have magnified how many different ways there were of *constructing* R.S. – with the press in England and Wales having very different ideas of who 'their R.S.' had been, bringing ever new 'Thomases' to life, posthumously – another uncanny phenomenon.

And from that point onwards, there were two pathways which R.S. laid open for me. There was the academic pathway, which kept me holed up in a tiny, dimly lit room at the top of Bangor University's library which then housed the R.S. Thomas Study Centre, and there were other, literal pathways, or shall we say footpaths – which took this unsuspecting 21-year-old girl from Ceredigion (fresh from the Norfolk Broads), and planted her deep in the north Walian landscape, a wholly unfamiliar terrain. Not until I arrived did I understand the importance of actually immersing myself in the very same landscape and living out the same geographical existence as R.S. By strange accident, I found myself living on Anglesey, the island where Thomas spent his childhood, the place he longed to return to throughout most of his life. I found myself in a cottage overlooking the Menai Straits – staring back at the young R.S., who, sixty years or so earlier, had found himself in lodgings in Bangor overlooking the same Menai Straits from the other direction. And I found, possibly as he had done, that it wasn't a view that was particularly conducive to academic work.

Like the young R.S., I went roaming. I discovered the solitude of Penmon, the beauty of Traeth Coch, the coppery planet of Mynydd Parys. I spent months trying to avoid my own work but didn't realise (perhaps until as I'm writing this) that all that time I was actually undertaking 'field work' on R.S., living my (very different) life in his (not so different) landscapes, and it deepened and enriched my experience of his work and of Wales – the Wales I felt I knew so well until I discovered, through him, that there was so much more of it to see.

Then, another signpost emerged. A notice in the paper advertising the post of a writer-in-residence on Bardsey Island. I had just been reading R.S. Thomas's poem 'Pilgrimages' and his essays on Bardsey in Welsh. As it was a place that had meant a great deal to him, the furthest-point-west-from-the-furthest-point-west, I felt that this was another opportunity that I could not let pass by, and in the summer of 2002 I landed on Bardsey as their first ever writer in residence. I had R.S.'s poems by my side at every opportunity, crawling along each inch of rock and sand with his words sloshing about in my head, waiting to discover the island-within-the-island that was R.S. Thomas. But of course, I discovered very little about him – for he was long gone, and no one on the island had much to say about him either. He had questioned in his poem 'Pilgrimages', whether he was too late to discover anything truly remarkable on Bardsey. And perhaps he was right in thinking that the pilgrims never really found what they were looking for, either. For the Bardsey I was searching for was not the one I found. In fact, I found a far more interesting one.

I gradually came to realise that, although R.S. had led me there, the experience was entirely my own. And the experience, of solitude, silence, of midnight bird-attractions and late-afternoon mountain-clambering, of soul-searching among like-minded people who were cut-adrift, all these things were enabling me to become a writer. After years of aspiring to become one, but feeling I had nothing to say, I'd finally found my first real subject to write about at length. Two novels followed – one in Welsh, *Atyniad*, and then, in English, *Twenty Thousand Saints*. Those texts undoubtedly launched my literary career, and did so bilingually, with one winning the Prose Medal at the Eisteddfod and the other winning the Oxfam Hay Emerging Writer's Prize at the Hay Festival. I have no doubt in my mind that without R.S. Thomas, neither book would exist.

Finally, after finishing my thesis, we went our separate ways. I tried to forget about him – pushing his head back over the half-door of Sarn y Plas in Rhiw, back into the darkness. But he came knocking. Or rather, I came knocking, at Sarn y Plas, and that half-door opened again.

I had spent almost a decade 'not knowing' R.S. Thomas, trying to find my own voice, and my own place as a bilingual writer. But then an invite came to write and present a documentary about R.S. for S4C, entitled *Pererindod R.S.*, an overview of Thomas's time in Pen Llŷn. Although I had spent time on Bardsey, Llŷn was still a new canvas to explore, and I relished having the opportunity to delve back into the field work. The focus was on re-discovering R.S. as genial neighbour and friend, and as a Welsh-speaker and campaigner. Porth Neigwl, Llanbedrog, Nefyn, Abersoch, and Uwch Mynydd became part of the backdrop – remarkable places I was discovering for the first time.

Although we were there to portray a poet, there were also moments of pure fiction. Having read that the writer Aled Jones Williams had burnt his cassock in a kind of 'copy-cat' burning of R.S.'s own (apocryphal) act, I decided it would be fitting to script an interview with Aled which dramatised this symbolic act. Poking the ashes as the sun set over Porth Colmon beach, Aled remarked, 'whether R.S. burnt his cassock or not, the fact is I did, and all because I'd heard he had done it.' As it was burning, it occurred to me that this was the point at which worlds collided and the boundaries blurred; I was inside a fiction about R.S. which was now of my own making, which, possibly, had been of his own making, too.

From then on, things fell almost too neatly into place. Sarn y Plas, once R.S. Thomas's home, was empty – or so we had been told. We passed by, more than once, meaning to come back and film the grounds.

But then a contributor told us he'd seen a light on in one of the windows. The next day someone else mentioned activity at Sarn y Plas, as though R.S. himself were back in town. Just as we were packing up to head back south, out of that famous half-door of Sarn y Plas came Gwydion Thomas, the poet's son, bringing to life a moment frozen in time. It was a moment I could never have scripted, and which, thankfully, made it into the documentary, in the form of a wonderfully frank and touching interview – one that will stay with me for a long time, and which granted me, for the first time, the opportunity to appreciate R.S. as a family man, as a father, and husband.

And this is how the girl who went into the east found herself wandering through the wild garden of the man who went into the west, wondering what on earth she was doing there. Just as he had once insisted that a house was not a dead thing, I found Sarn y Plas reverberating with life, with Gwydion making dinner at the kitchen table and Elodie, his daughter, reading in another room – there was the sense of life having taken place there; *still* taking place there. For the first time, I felt deeply connected to R.S.'s world. And the connection was forever sealed, in the form of a small booklet Gwydion slipped into my hand just as I was leaving. A copy of *In her Ashen Studio*, a private, handmade collection of R.S. and Elsi's works, set beautifully side by side, on Japanese Papers. I was deeply touched by this gesture, and spent many days afterwards poring over it – reading the meaningful dedications, appreciating the art anew. For the first time, I felt something real and tangible had come into my possession that had come directly from R.S. himself; something no library or archive or study centre would have been able to give me.

It was a moment that made me feel that, unlike those Bardsey pilgrims, perhaps I was not too late, after all.

R.S. and the £1 Notes

Gillian Clarke

In the 1970s, Yr Academi Gymreig, English Language Section (a clumsy, if accurate, title), held a conference at Gregynog. It was my first attendance at such an event. My first collection, *Snow on the Mountain*, had just been published as one of the Triskel series, and Meic Stephens, its editor and editor of *Poetry Wales*, where my early poems first appeared, suggested I should attend. I had been at home with young children for about eight years, now an excited new member of the Academi, a nervous newcomer to the Welsh literary scene, meeting Welsh writers – meeting any writers – for the first time. The visitor on Saturday night was R.S. Thomas.

I had no idea what to expect of that first encounter with the man himself. My studies of poetry at school and in university were almost entirely of the Great Dead, all of them men, and English. The subliminal message from education in the 1950s and '60s told us that English Poetry was poetry written by Great Dead Englishmen. I discovered *Poetry Wales* and my first contemporary poem at about the same time, ten years after university, when I had three young children and no career. The journal was intriguing, and showed me there were new ways to write poetry, but the discovered poem was a bolt to the heart. It was 'The Cat and the Sea', by R.S. Thomas, of whom I had never heard. Having read all the greats from Anglo-Saxon poetry through Chaucer to the Romantics, and not much published since, I found this short poem, just six lines, a revelation. It was a spell. Words turned the sea and the gorse-clad cliff into a cat, and, more wonderfully, the cat into the sea, so succinctly that I read it over and over to see how the trick was done. How did ordinary words somewhere in the poem's lines – but where? – transubstantiate one thing into another? And why did that make my heart beat faster, my skin tingle? When the new poetry freed my own work from the secrecy of the private notebook, it was R.S. who unlocked it.

At the conference in Gregynog, I stood in the meeting room and was introduced to him. He was jovial – I choose my word with care – his accent strangely grand and English. He shook my hand and made a joke to those standing in the group, among them Raymond Garlick, I think, and Roland Mathias, about poetry being with the young ones now. His reading that night, and the poems, are with me still.

Some time in the late 1970s, I was invited by the Head of Llantarnam Comprehensive School, Cwmbrân, to be poet-in-residence for two terms. A recently converted secondary modern, deprived of the lift provided by all those eleven-years-olds creamed off for the local grammar school, and the attention they would have demanded of their teachers, it was left with an unambitious English Department and the Head, Russell Cooper, thought a poet might provide the inspiration his pupils needed. I thought so too, so I decided to invite some of our best poets to visit the school (Dannie Abse, among others). I began with R.S. Thomas. I wrote to him, inviting him to come and read to the staff and the students at Llantarnam, suggesting I meet his train at Newport, and I offered to accommodate him overnight at my house in Cardiff. I am astonished, now, at my impertinence. However, a few days later, the phone rang and my twelve-year-old son, Dylan, answered, turned to me, shocked, and whispered, 'It's R.S. Thomas!' Down the line came his sonorous voice saying: 'Thursday would suit me best. Thank you, yes, I will stay with you.'

He arrived at Newport station and I drove him to school in my Renault 4. He had to fold himself up to fit into it. I was wracked by anxiety about driving safely, talking sensibly, giving him due respect. The room was full of young people, among them those who had failed the now abolished 11-plus, and been designated 'not grammar school material'. They were entranced. The excellent Head, Russell Cooper, was present, and other members of his staff, from the Departments of History, French, Religious Studies and PE (I had to adjust my prejudices against PE teachers at Llantarnam), as well as the school cleaner and others too numerous to mention. From the English Department only one came, a new, young teacher who later rose to a deservedly senior post in the University of Newport. R.S. read in his thrillingly deep voice as if he were preaching to the waves on the beach at Aberdaron. No doubt he sounded 'posh' to the students, but they believed him, knew him for the real poet he was, though they had never before been offered his or any other great poetry in their classrooms. Then they asked their naïve questions, which he answered without a hint of that 'curmudgeonliness' of which he has so often been accused. They loved him, and there are some, I know, who remember the event to this day. Then he accompanied some of the staff to the pub. He drank water.

I drove him home, where my two sons, aged twelve and fourteen, were at the door to meet us, on their best behaviour. I introduced them and said nervously, fearing an imperfectly tidied house, especially as I had assigned him Owain's bedroom, 'Owain and Dylan have prepared the house for you'. Before stepping through the front door, R.S. looked around as one who surveys the horizon for the sight of a distant sail, and said: 'I see no red carpet!' The boys loved it. A great poet who made jokes! While I prepared a meal in the kitchen, they talked in the living room. I heard laughter. Next day the boys told me R.S. said he could not help thinking, while in the pulpit, of the similarity between the words 'God' and 'Cod', and he would imagine a great fish leaping from the waves to greet him with the voice of God/Cod.

Next morning I drove him to the station. The boys walked to school. When I got back I found an envelope on Owain's pillow which read: 'R.S. was 'ere'. In it were two pound notes, one each. Pound notes! That seems a long time ago.

I recall Meic Stephens telling me that his daughter and her friend, students at Bangor, had called on R.S. in his cottage in Aberdaron, and had been given a scoop – an exclusive interview for the university magazine. Such stories run counter to the gossip about his remoteness and rudeness, and I never witnessed that curmudgeonly mood. In almost every story of his acts of kindness, young people were the beneficiaries. He could be good to poets too. When his wife, the painter Mildred Eldridge, died, I wrote to him. I had exchanged a few brief letters with him over the years, always to request a reading, or to thank him for one. His were formal notes, usually ending 'R.S.'. His reply to my letter of condolence was more giving. He allowed himself to say more than usual, to admit grief, and this time he signed his name, 'Ronald'.

I once met a man who told me he had visited Eglwys-fach while researching the poet and his work for a PhD. He spoke to the locals in the pub, and they looked blank. He talked about his research, asked about the man. Suddenly one of the locals slapped the bar and said, 'You mean the Mr Thomas, the vicar!' They did not think of him as a famous writer, but reported that he was a good minister, attending to the sick or visiting a death-bed with due kindness. As for his poetry, they knew not a word of it.

Years ago R.S. gave a memorable reading with Sorley Maclean in Cardiff. Ned Thomas, my husband David Thomas and I were tasked with taking them out for a meal. It was, I think, in an Italian restaurant in one of the streets off St Mary Street. R.S. loved Scottish airs, and the poetry of Burns, so the conversation between him and Sorley was rich and dancing with quotes and stories. For me the most powerful image of the evening was of their two great heads leaning towards each other against golden light from an illuminated tank of ornamental fish just behind them, and R.S.'s head haloed by the flickering, translucent ribbons of the gills of an angel fish.

When one year R.S. gave one of his rare readings to a packed marquee at Hay, the applause from the Festival audience was long and warm. As I stepped into the aisle to leave I found myself beside a well-known London poet, 'H.W.'. I sensed a sneer coming. He said: 'What did you think of that?' Me: 'Marvellous.' He: 'Oh! We didn't think much of it.' Me: 'But listen to the audience!' He: 'That just confirms my view, and "B.M." [another London poet] agrees with me.'

Before the reading R.S. was interviewed on Radio Wales and the dialogue went like this. Interviewer: 'You have often been invited to Hay. What made you accept the invitation this time?' R.S.: 'Oh, the money!' In fact, Hay does not pay writers to perform. It assumes the publisher will compensate the writer. Later, at a reception, my husband, David, asked R.S., conspiratorially: 'You say you did it for the money! How much did they pay you?' 'Double figures!' he replied.

At an event in Cardiff in the '90s, I noted, nervously, that R.S. was in the room where I was about to give a reading. I spoke to him, and he introduced me to someone I had recently seen in his company at Hay. Betty – Elisabeth Vernon – who would become his second wife. She was charming, friendly, small and brightly stylish with red painted nails. She remembered me from an event at Presteigne, where we had both been sponsors of a local festival. R.S. said, 'We live in Presteigne now.' We? Uncertain of what he was telling me, I responded, 'Don't you miss the sea?' 'Yes,' he replied, 'but the company is marvellous.' He and Betty smiled at each other. I realised I had been given important news. No one else, it seemed, when I quietly questioned those I thought should know, had been told. R.S. was now with Betty, close to her disabled daughter who was, I believe, in a residential home nearby. In his old age he had found a new love. Extraordinary!

I loved the early work for its simplicity and strength, but I never enjoyed his Iago Prytherch poems, his peasant gobbing in the fire, 'the vacancy of his mind'. Coming from farming people myself, I objected to such a reduction of farmers to 'peasants'. Yet I could see there was, even in such poems, always a moment of glory, a 'halleluiah', the bright field in the dark of a rain-besieged landscape, a moment of sunlight after rain, and the peasant is described as a 'winner of wars', his mind enflamed by the same small star as lights us all home.

I always loved, too, his simple opening words in the form of a question: 'You remember Davies?', and, much later, in 'Zero', the common question, 'What time is it?' is answered with a roll-call of myths and heroes, Pharaoh and the baby in the bullrushes, Dido and Aenaeus, Caesar, and Aneirin's great poem. And so on through cultural history to a devastating final line. The poem is a triumph, retaining his early characteristics of starting with a simple question or statement.

It is now his later poems I most admire, poems of the sea, of bird-watching, of God's absence and presence, the warmth he feels in the empty form of the hare.

Yes, he could be 'curmudgeonly'. I like the word, so let us give him credit for inhabiting it so splendidly when he liked. He was also quick with a witticism and very funny, and, as Menna Elfyn has said, he was the thorn in the conscience of Wales at the time when we needed it, when we were too ready to please, to give up our language in the name of good manners, in the name of welcome, yielding to a newcomer at the drop of a Croeso cynnes.

A year before he died, we spoke at an event in Portmeirion. He told me he was not well, but stood, tall and strong, belying the news, and giving no details when I responded with my concern. We know great men die, but we don't believe it. In the case of poets we are right not to believe it. Is Shakespeare dead? Is Dafydd ap Gwilym dead? Is Dante dead? Their poems are who they are, and they speak as long as language lives, and that must be good enough.

A year later, in September 2000, as I switched on the radio in my room in a gloomy hotel in Middlesborough, I heard that he had died. I couldn't sleep, so I wrote. It is quicker, more apt if, rather than tell it again, I conclude this account with the short elegy I wrote that night.

RS

His death
on the midnight news.
Suddenly colder.

Gold September's driven off
by something afoot
in the south-west approaches.

God's breathing in space out there
misting the heave of the sea
dark and empty tonight,

except for the one frail coracle
borne out to sea,
burning.

The Ornithologist-Poet as a Bird

Osi Rhys Osmond

There was something of the raptor about R.S. Thomas and although the gift of physical flight had passed him by he was capable from his lofty metaphysical eminence of taking in the whole of Wales, and much beyond. As I began to read and experience the poetry and the poet I realised that walking and watching was as critical to his output as his poetic vision and that a greater appreciation of his work might be gained by becoming familiar with the significant habitats of his long creative life. In his three parishes and in his retirement at Rhiw he seems to personify four distinct phases of bird-like character and as he moves there is change, a change in the poetry and a change in the man: places affected him deeply, partly from expectation and subsequent disappointment and partly from the new reality; there is an overlap, what is nascent in one location comes to fruition in the next, until that new location begins to dominate his imagination.

It seems as though the birdwatcher becomes the watching bird; the hunting bird – the beak, feathers, wings, flight, freedom and containment, echo throughout his work. He begins in Manafon as a hawk, patrolling the bleak uplands, becomes a stalking harrier on the marshes and against the buttress of Foel Fawr at Eglwys-fach, stoops like a falcon from the sea-cliff parish of Aberdaron and becomes the majestic sea-eagle of Llŷn in his most productive creative home, the cottage at Rhiw where he lived until shortly before his death in 2000.

In 2013, the centenary year of the birth of the poet I began working on a series of fairly large, mixed media works on paper – 'graphic essays' or 'graphic psycho-geography' is how I originally described this method of working; drawing, mapping, collaging, writing and layering past and present – examining the poetry, life and landscapes of R.S. Thomas. In order to do so, although I had met the poet on various occasions in the last twenty or so years of his life, I visited and revisited the three major parishes of his ministry as an Anglican clergyman, and his retirement cottage on the Llŷn. I made drawings, spoke to people, watched birds, studied the landscape and maps, wrote and took photographs.

These places have changed considerably since R.S. Thomas ministered to his parishioners, as have the parishioners, but nature and the physical landscape – the hills, fields, woods, moors, rivers, mountains, cliffs and sea – remain much the same. Whether one can effectively explore and/or interpret poetry (or more accurately the poetic impulse) by visual means is perhaps a controversial issue and one that I will leave the viewers of the works to resolve for themselves. The most important of these locations as far as his poetic output is concerned was his final metaphysical parish of Rhiw, a short distance, but quite separate from, the village of the same name.

The social and physical environments of our formative years are acknowledged to be a powerful influence on our development. In the case of the artist, whatever the art form, that environment, together with his or her immediate physical surroundings, can be crucial in determining the creative urge, focusing both the form and content of the work.

It was in the parish of Manafon that he first became located in one place for an extended period and much of the poetry he wrote there reflects the immediate environs of his ministry. The hill farmers were his parishioners and he chose them as the primary subject of his work. There were other parishioners farming much richer and more productive land along the valley floor, but they did not interest him in the same way, nor, it seems, did the villagers. In choosing the hard, stark, outsider existence of the hill farmers he engaged with an almost eremitic way of life which reflected his own innate tenaciousness.

It was a poem from this place and period that provided one of my most memorable encounters with the work of R.S. Thomas, very soon after I had begun teaching art in a west Wales secondary school. That year, in the early Seventies the Urdd Eisteddfod had a painting competition that featured the poem 'Cynddylan on a Tractor'. It may not be generally considered one of his major works, but it spurred the imaginations and identified the longings of many of my pupils, especially those country boys who felt imprisoned by school and couldn't wait to leave and take their place on the family farm.

The R.S. Thomas we hear about is often portrayed as a sour, unyielding, humourless man, bitter perhaps and certainly unsympathetic, but as they read his poem he spoke to those children as a joyous bringer of meaning, their family's lives and their own ambitions personified in a poem, and in my experience of his company this was closer to the truth of the man. Thomas seemed to be a real presence in the art-room, that year. Describing the impact of modern agricultural machinery on Welsh rural life, its delights and dangers, and one simple man's reaction to these developments, the poem also alludes to Thomas's anxiety about mechanisation as he describes Cynddylan almost as a 'cefn gwlad' Don Quixote, tilting at the questionable progress that will stain the purity of his peasant soul.

Over the following years I met R.S. Thomas on a number of occasions, conversing with him, generally in English, always socially, and usually at his poetry readings, or as part of some public demonstration protesting against nuclear weapons, marching in favour of self-government for Wales. His general demeanour, although severe and somewhat dour, hid a mischievous, passionate and humorous man of great warmth.

Walking beside Thomas one was able to engage in conversation with him in a way that might not have been possible in a more formal context – the forward motion of the crowd, the commonality of purpose creating a unifying camaraderie in which normal boundaries of discourse melted away. He was, obviously, a serious man, and like many creative people deadly serious, but he was certainly not miserable. He was alert to everything around him; he noticed the smallest things. He would comment on the police presence, the depressingly small size of the crowd which confirmed his disappointment with Wales and the Welsh; he was critical of those who purported to lead us, noting who was present and remarking on significant absences. He was observant of people and of what they wore, their 'plumage' as fascinating to him as that of his birds. He reacted favourably to the proximity of beauty and was not averse to discreetly remarking on the physical charms of individuals.

In his poem 'On Hearing a Welshman Speak' he writes of a praying girl and how even in a sacred place the thoughts of the flesh arise impetuously. The dangers of our natural biological drive he compares to the instinctive insistence of the hawk's eye; he neatly excuses himself, however, by placing himself at one remove in the persona of the mediaeval poet, Dafydd ap Gwilym, who expressed similar thoughts in some of his poems.

The reference to the predatory falcon reinforces our idea of Thomas's hawk-like gaze which intensified with age in photographs that appeared to confirm his supposedly irascible nature, serving at the same time to establish and reinforce his reputation as an austere poetic force, sharp-beaked, talons bared, lofty and unapproachable.

While we marched together, Thomas expressed his views and canvassed mine on the subject of the rally, often returning to the question of the inmigration of English-speakers and what this meant for the language, or the indifference of the Welsh as to the fate of their culture; we never talked about birds.

To walk and talk with Thomas was an experience I shall never forget; he walked with the easy gait of the moorland shepherd; he was vigorous and he was vigilant; and, as I had come to expect, caustic, cautionary and compelling, his words formulated within a physical frame which by then was an external manifestation of the inner workings of his mind – he *looked* like his poems, or perhaps he looked like the only man capable of making that poetry. From his early days he had been athletic, something which still manifested itself despite the onset of old age. The people in Thomas's poetry, particularly the peasants, conform to a lean type and if you want to find the man, to see his silhouette, you will find him there, striding the bleak moors.

If here, as a hawk, he hovered over the hills of Powys, he ranged harrier-like from lowland Eglwys-fach with the vast bulwark of Foel Fawr behind him and the wild spaces of Cors Fochno before him. His ornithological passions were reinforced here by the rich diversity of habitat. He met fellow enthusiasts and he met people he would rather not have met – certain English inmigrants. He was surprised by their presence and their inability to sense what he saw as the precarious state of the Welsh language and culture and how their presence exacerbated the already parlous situation. While socialising with and ministering to them, his Christian charity was severely tested and by his own admission, found wanting. His words reflected this – we see a new impatience breaking through. Many of the poems from his early Eglwys-fach years, however, are unfinished upland business – poems that were mere beginnings, inchoate in Manafon, emerging absolute in lowland Eglwys-fach.

In Aberdaron Thomas's poetry began to reflect the characteristics of this windswept, rocky coastal parish from whose church he could sense the proximity and significance of Ynys Enlli, the island of saints. Here he becomes the falcon, the peregrine, that most implacable of birds, as he became the most implacable and steadfast of poets. The curiously metallic cry of the peregrine is the closest thing in nature to the crisp, pared reading voice of the poet.

When I met him during this period it was usually at poetry readings in Cardiff or Swansea. During these readings I always had a small drawing book in front of me and made numerous, rapid drawings as Thomas read; listening and drawing enabled me to see Thomas as a physical being and even as a landscape of his own making.

If he had told the audience with his wry smile and mischievous demeanour that he had flown or swooped down under his own power, airborne from the north, I for one would have believed him. To hear him read, his frame hunched over the lectern, was an extraordinary experience. Recordings give us something of the flavour of his voice and intonation, but they can never carry the power of his physical presence or the way he moved the air before him. Most memorably, I once heard him read at the Park Hotel in Cardiff in the early Nineties. The audience was spellbound, hushed and silent, as Thomas read poems he had typed out on the lightest foolscap paper he could find. I don't know if this was the way he always typed or presented his poetry, but I'd never experienced anything quite like this in his other readings. As he began to read, the words left his mouth like stainless steel knives, they spun towards us, absolutely on target, swishing, sharp, precise, relentless, razor-like: as if, to paraphrase the poet, keened on a cloud's lip.

The sound he projected was more than music, it was meaning. His voice was like the paper, rasping, desiccated, and raptor-like; it tore mercilessly, but slowly, through the air, his message was intense, but his words were light, they took flight and he read with the impeccable focus and timing of the knife-thrower. The paper was released directly in front of him as each poem came to an end, allowing the cushion of warm air and gravity to carry it gently down to the table's surface to rest lightly upon the other poems. It was extremely thin paper, brittle, white and weightless and as it wafted slowly down it moved from side to side, carving an eloquent hiss out of the air. As the final words were spoken, still spinning outwards over our heads, the last sheet descended, coming to rest with perfect synchronicity, as weary with us as the poet himself while the closing words of the concluding poem faded from his lips.

From his ultimate parish, the spartan cottage at Rhiw, sheltering on the leeward side of the Llŷn, overlooking the boiling waters of Porth Neigwl, the poet, hawk-like and buffeted by life's harsh winds, gazed out, quartering the broad bay, watching the weather's abrupt changes of mood as he waited for his beloved, inspirational birds to pass, reliable almost, yet still erratic; evanescent beings as elusive as his often absent God. This was the poetic parish he served longest, and from here he looked more deeply and flew still higher, his work soaring outwards and upwards as he contemplated humanity, matter, and faith; the earth, the universe; time, space, and what lay beyond.

R.S. Thomas and I

or how we drew near and how the most miserable man since Leonard Cohen turned my work from barely influenced by Wales and its endless matters to the hardest of hard core

Peter Finch

It's 1962 and those of us in the vanguard have been down to H.J. Lears and bought the first manifestation of British poetry's new popularity, *Penguin Modern Poets* No. 1. A paperback publishing first, its smart black and white cover wrapping 115 pages of the kind of stuff most around me would rather leave the country to avoid than read. Modern verse. Described in the blurb's sans serif face as 'an attempt to introduce contemporary poetry to the general reader'. Two and six, just about affordable, if I gave up a night in the Moulders Arms. Each Penguin volume would feature three poets from the cutting edge. Number One had Lawrence Durrell of *The Black Book*, Elizabeth Jennings from the Movement and an arcane-sounding Welsh vicar at the height of his Iago Prytherch period, R.S. Thomas.

This was the British answer to James Laughlin's New Directions publishing and Lawrence Ferlinghetti's City Lights Books. I imagined it to be this. The new place from which British verse would launch itself into the pockets and bags of a hip new generation of British revolutionaries who would, as the Sixties rolled, turn the social and cultural landscape of the UK into something utterly new. Durrell, Jennings and Thomas might not be quite the most appropriate harbingers of the forthcoming revolution but, for now, they'd have to do. Durrell I'd come across via my readings of Henry Miller, Elizabeth Jennings through Amis and Larkin. But R.S. was something new.

Poems about Prytherch, cold darkness, wet fields and suffering pain. It was all so downhearted, so deeply dark and so depressing. Thomas depicted a Wales with which I was totally unfamiliar. A depopulated upland, rich with relics, crowded with empty fields, and its past brittle with ghosts. A soft, misused, underused, threatened language hung across it like a miasma. There was nowhere to go. Even the poet himself had given up. It was all in vain, he declared. I turned to Leonard Cohen to cheer me up.

But R.S. had got there. He'd wormed his way into my subconscious. This despite his formality, his clear use of language, his unwillingness to follow trend, his rejection of modernism, modernity, in fact almost anything to do with the contemporary world. Where the Sixties were at was not Thomas's Wales. The Sixties had little to do with the people Thomas wrote about. Prytherch, not the brightest in creation, working on menial tasks in the fields, smelling of animals, full of sweat and stain.

The poet would, I was to learn later, wander the same fields that he described, marked with the same upland hedgerows, and seeing others approach, often his own parishioners, would vault the greenery and hide. He did this lest human engagement would punch a hole in his creative flow. A man after my own heart. In part, it would seem.

But what I was doing was something else. I was building a new, young consensus. Starting a revolutionary and far reaching literary magazine, engaging in public poetry performances, turning verse from its home on the quiet lectern to a vibrant new force at loose in the air. I wanted to see the Wales around me rich with new influences, shifting dynamically as the age progressed. Thomas was at the heart of a tradition that valued unchanging certainty and the values of convention above most else. When I produced an issue of my new magazine, *second aeon*, which, in its editorial matter, contained not a single capital letter the Welsh arts funding establishment had apoplexy. Bauhaus be damned, this barbarism cannot be allowed to prevail. Who does he think he is? Is he Welsh?

I was, not that this made much difference in a Welsh literary world where almost everything rested on how much of the past you could stuff inside your verse. Down there, at the Reardon Smith Lecture Hall in Cardiff, I sat and listened to the poet Harri Webb. Webb, a poet I was to come to know and to admire greatly as a pungent and able chronicler of our collective fate, and a humourist par excellence in nationalist circles, was that day on stage bleating about loss and exile. Mountain Ash, where he worked as a librarian, was so far from London that you felt in exile every time you travelled to that city, he told us. Hiraeth, he claimed, would hold you only to be satisfied by your swift and immediate return. Wales in its glowing, rain-swept green wonder, was everything. The world beyond was a dismal and unimportant place.

He sat down and was followed by John Idris Jones who read about the fairground at Barry Island and then by Roland Mathias who recited stern and difficult poetry which recalled Welsh historical events. Where was John Cage in all this? Eugen Gomringer and the concrete poets? Allen Ginsberg? Jackson Mac Low, Henri Chopin, the Liverpool bards, Peter Redgrove, Charles Bukowski, Gary Snyder, Charles Olson, Ed Dorn, Robert Creeley, Guillaume Appolinaire, Jack Spicer, Frank O'Hara, Louis Zukofsky, Denise Levertov, Tom Raworth, Gertrude Stein, William Carlos Williams, Bob Cobbing?

Nowhere. We lived in the barren lands. There was no place for those poets here.

I took Thomas's 'Welsh Landscape' with its blood in the skies and its inbred, impotent people and made it my own. 1966. 'A Welsh Wordscape'. A young man's fight back. I felt like the man who alone confronted the tanks in Tiananmen Square. But Roland Mathias, then editor of *Anglo-Welsh Review*, liked it enough to publish it. I sent a copy to R.S. He did not respond.

Not replying, I was to learn, was how things were with R.S. For me anyway.

R.S., despite his non-engagement with most of the things I held dear, had seeped into my blood. My obsession with his work arriving slowly, by osmosis. Pretty much as Flann O'Brien has it in *The Third Policeman* where the atoms of the iron bicycle and those of the cycle's rider become one through constant close proximity. Open my vein and in there among the theories of random creation and the permanent dada revolution would be a small but discernible trace of Thomas's singular but spiritual Welsh depression. Finch the verse futurologist dabbling with tradition, with that which had gone before.

In 1982 I bought my first computer. This was a cassette-powered

BBC B with a memory about as large as a present-day talking greeting card but revolutionary for the time. I learned Basic, the BBC's simple programming language, and worked out how you could make the machine generate poetry of its own. I established a number of data sources and asked the machine to construct lines by taking words at random from each pool and, after inserting appropriate links, offering them as new pieces of verse. This was pretty much what Tristan Tzara had done when he cut up sentences and drew their constituent words one by one from a top hat. That was back in the dada days of the early 1920s. Only my version did the trick with speed, and with polish and involved human intervention not at all.

For my data I used the books of R.S. I spent days scouring his work, sucking out verbs and adjectives and entering them into memory. The new lines emerged by the thousand. 'Abominations break above the river... the nation majestically watered.' I toyed with the idea of submitting the best under a nom de plume to *Poetry Wales* but settled for sending copies directly to the great man. As ever he did not reply.

In 1976 we'd met when the Charles Street Oriel Bookshop, which at that time I managed, released *R.S. Thomas Reading His Own Poems*, a 12-inch vinyl album of the poet's greatest hits. The launch had been so packed that women fainted and had to be passed to the exit over the heads of the crowd football-terrace style. There had been huge expectation and a considerable amount of cheering. The poet appeared unmoved, read from his work, signed album sleeves when asked and then left as soon as possible. Julian Shepard took a photograph of R.S. and me; me long-haired and full of the future, R.S. pulling his chin pretending he didn't know me at all.

This sense of detachment and of being unmoved by fame and unfazed by great crowds became an R.S. characteristic. In 1989 he appeared on stage at the Sherman Theatre reading as part of the Cardiff Literature Festival. The event was chaired by Ned Thomas and performing alongside R.S. was his great Scots Gaelic rival, Sorley Maclean. In relation to the Celtic languages of their respective countries the two occupied comparable positions. R.S. baulking at the decline of indigenous Welsh, Maclean angered by the dilution of his native Gaelic.

Maclean read first and gave a rousing, chest-banging, uproarious performance. performance. R.S. sat through it in stillness. Not a muscle twitched for a whole 30 minutes. He sat expressionless, head down, legs crossed. I wondered if he were in deep meditation or even unaccountably dead. But when the Maclean express train and the cheering had stopped the priest rose slowly to his feet and began to untie his bundle of books. These were strung together in a stack as books might have been in the 1930s. He worked as if he were a performing magician, untangling the string and then pedantically rolling it up and storing it in his pocket. He must have taken several minutes to complete the task and not once did he look at his audience. In our hundreds we sat there in great expectation. Would R.S. perhaps pull a rabbit from his jacket or balance his volumes on his head and set them spinning? Instead he read without commentary and with barely a pause between poems. He used his then latest set, *Experimenting with an Amen*. The verse was dark, slow, and unchallengeable.

He finishes. The darkness returns. The audience applaud and leave. They go home and, like me, reach for their Leonard Cohen albums. Except that singer was now no longer fashionable.

R.S. you are in my blood. If you'd been a blues singer then this is how your cyclopaedia entry would read:

> *RNLD TOMOS (vcl, hca, some prse) aka Curtis Langdon. 1913-2000. Gospel. Austerity tradition. Jnd Iago Prytherch Big Band (1959), gog, gap, bwlch, lleyn, tan, iaith, mynydd, mangle, adwy – mainly on Hart-Davis race label. Reissue Dent PoBkSoc Special Recommnd. Concert at Sherman support Sorley Maclean (gtr, hrt clutching) sold out. Fire Bomb tour Sain triple cd for D Walford Davies (vcl, crtcl harmonium) new century highspot. A pioneer of dark wounds and internal tensions. In old age bird song and reliable grouch. Stood, was counted, still no change. To live in Wales is to become un-assailable. 'An angel-fish' (Clarke). Expect retrospective, marvelling and statue.*

Obsessions need outlets. In the early 1990s I launched an R.S. Thomas website. As an antidote to the wild expressionism of things that had gone before I kept its title as plain as I could: *R.S. Thomas Information*. Not a hint in that title of what it really was. I wanted to extend my ideas from the BBC computer experiments a decade or more earlier and, in the process, immerse myself in the work of my chosen, distant, and miserable mentor. A man of the people. So long as you spoke the tongue.

I dredged through the *Collected Poems*, deconstructed its content, reassembled, restructured, retook, and then ordered what I'd revealed. I added loops of cross reference, hunted the net for lists of influences, both on and by, detailed fellow travellers, critics, associates, authors whose work intersected, styles, traits. I compiled and extended. Politicians who he'd admired, philosophers he'd been influenced by. Men of the cloth who'd travelled paths like his. His editors. His enemies. His friends. Things they'd said of him. Positions they'd held.

Visitors to the ever expanding site began to respond. They'd look R.S. Thomas up on Yahoo. My *R.S. Thomas Information* was one of the results. It sounded real enough although what most thought when they visited I have no idea. When replies arrived I often incorporated them. I free formed and imagined how I and others might have related to the blues singer, the poet, the Welsh visionary, the saviour of the uplands, the man of god and the champion of the Welshness of Wales.

These slabs of information formed and reformed. They gained a postmodern fluidity which had no place in the original work. I wanted, if I could, to present R.S. metadata, the lode from which his poetry had sprung. Somewhere among it would be an R.S. epicentre, a place from where all he was ebbed and flowed. Did I write and tell him I was making this thing? Given my experiences down the years (Can you read at our festival? No reply), refusal (Would you like to contribute to my magazine? No), dislike (What do you think of this new promotional postcard of you I've published? I think it should be withdrawn), and absolute distrust of anything in the south (Could I invite you to Cardiff? Sorry, my audience is elsewhere) I decided I wouldn't bother.

My RST web presence blossomed. The R.S. Thomas Study Centre

at Bangor and any number of other academically-based R.S. Thomas data sources were yet to go online. For a time I had the World Wide Web to myself.

In Cardiff Bay, BT were building an internet data centre – a new century data farm and high security storage facility for commercial and financial online records. Three data halls, 12,000 servers. Black and chrome. Security fenced. Guards. They needed a piece of appropriate art to decorate their fortress structure's façade. They chose an adapted version of my R.S. Thomas Information. His poetry and his influences, deconstructed and reassembled, now ran across the building's frontage, through its entrance doors and along its corridors.

R.S. Thomas, arguably Wales's greatest poet, had arrived. His work now flowed among the binary numbers that defined our nation's financial and functional essence. Okay Ronald, you may not have liked my methods but I've now welded you into the digital future. Did you want to be here? If I had to guess then I imagine you'd say no.

R.S. Thomas: The Books

Jeff Towns

There is as yet no comprehensive bibliography of the writings and publications of R.S. Thomas, although various scholars and critics have made inroads into the task. The work was begun back in the Seventies by Sandra Anstey which culminated in her PhD thesis, *A Bibliography of the Poetry of R.S. Thomas* (1980). It is described thus:

> *Section 1 of Part 2 of this thesis consists of an alphabetical list of 606 poems by R.S. Thomas, up to and including 1978. In Section 2, each poem appears under the year and title of its first appearance as provided in the alphabetical list.*

The work has been carried on by Anstey and by those working at the R.S. Thomas Study centre in Bangor. Writing on the Oxford Bibliographies website Damian Walford Davies sums up the current position thus:

> *A complete bibliography of R.S. Thomas's published works will not be possible until the* Uncollected Poems, *currently in preparation, appears. A Complete Poems is planned. Anstey 1980 and Harris 1994 together offer inventories of the poetry up to 1993, as Harris 1994, Anstey and Walford Davies 2009 do for the published prose works up to the poet's death. Anstey, Harris 1994, Brown 1995-2007, Gramich 2008-, and Walford Davies 2009 collectively offer an inclusive list of critical writings up to 2003.*

I am in no position in this essay to offer anything to improve this completeness, after all I am a bookseller not a scholar, but I hope to point out some of the rarities and bibliographic curiosities in R.S.'s cannon. I also want to look at the books as physical objects and see how this reflects R.S. Thomas's view of himself and his writings, and how readers come to his work. I was taken, many years ago, by an essay in *Planet* by my friend John Harris, in which he looked at the books of Caradoc Evans, particularly *My People* from this perspective, and as someone who deals in books, it is an approach that appeals to me.

I am a bookseller with the strong, bordering on the obsessional, instincts of a mad collector. I have managed in some ways to sublimate this throughout my forty-five years trading by always having a collection or two on the go. The building of these extensive author and subject collections keeps my own desires to collect, *per se*, in check. I am known mostly for specialising in the work of Dylan Thomas, and have had a hand in building the collections of his works and manuscripts in Kyoto University in Japan, in The Dylan Thomas Centre in Swansea and more recently at the National Library of Wales. But the first significant collection I built was of Mervyn Peake, followed by, even if I say so myself, a fine Edward Thomas collection. These were eventually sold on, as were the collections of books on Gypsies (but I have started again!), books on Rock 'n' Roll and Fine Welsh Topographical Tours. Currently I have several collections on the go – Books on Tattooing, and collections of books and papers by Bruce Chatwin and Iain Sinclair – and Richard Brautigan – and R.S. Thomas.

The R.S. Thomas collection has been an ongoing, but slightly off-and-on project, going back over many years, and my holdings have often been raided when I felt compelled to offer rarities and bibliographical curiosities to Bangor, sometimes even gently bullied to do so!

R.S. Thomas is an interesting writer bibliographically and therefore of interest to a bookseller like myself and to collectors with imagination. His career spans many decades, his early poems came out in the plethora of literary magazines that sprang up in the UK in the Thirties, died out with the paper shortages of the War years, but blossomed again much later in the Sixties with the explosion of small press poetry 'zines' (many of them fabricated at home on makeshift duplicators and stapled together) that flourished in America and the UK. Many of these poems were then published in one of the annual poetry anthologies which used to appear, or would get included in themed anthologies (R.S. would later edit a few of these himself). Finally they would come out in one of the poet's own collections. Add to this scarce proof copies, the prose books and publications in Welsh, the fine limited editions of poems from Gwasg Gregynog, the Chilmark Press, and Kevin Perryman's productions from his German imprint Babel, not forgetting a few recordings on LP, cassette and CD, and the diligent completist collector has a rich and varied trove to pursue. That just leaves ephemera, iconography, newspaper articles, reviews and the curios, and the ever growing number of critical studies and biographies that the author's long writing life has thrown up.

I have yet to find any school magazines containing juvenile R.S. poems, and although I have read that while at university in Bangor he contributed to the college magazine under a pseudonym, these too have so far evaded me. I live in hope that some will turn up early one cold wintry Saturday morning at a small Cymdeithas Bob Owen Book Fair in deepest darkest Mold. The earliest periodicals I have handled are copies of the *Dublin Magazine* and the early appearances in Cyril Connolly's *Horizon*, Robert Herring's *Life and Letters* and Keidrych Rhys's *Wales*. The task of compiling a complete bibliography will no doubt be forthcoming from Bangor before too long, but odd little magazines and offbeat contributions are hard to track down and, when one reads something like this from the poet Gillian Clarke, 'I remember hearing him read a very amusing poem about hitching a lift, and flirting with the driver's wife in the windscreen mirror. It was full of wit and double entendre. I have not found it published anywhere', one begins to get the measure of the task.

So what follows here is a somewhat subjective selection of images and descriptions which seek to illuminate the richness and variety of R.S. Thomas's bibliography, a history which encompasses everything from tiny pamphlets to magnificent finely bound volumes and sees the great poet linked up with pulp-fiction 'biker' novels and children's books featuring gambolling baby goats!

R.S. Thomas's first book:

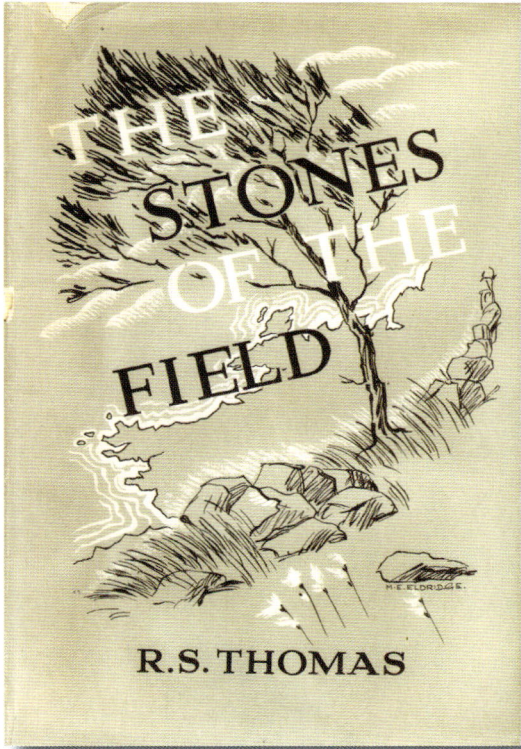

The Stones of the Field. The Druid Press Carmarthen. 1946. Published by Keidrych
Rhys at his Carmarthen-based press. (It was situated on Lammas Street, above Mr
Baugh's chip-shop). R.S. apparently paid £60 towards the cost of producing the edition.
The book was priced at six shillings and few copies are said to have been sold. The
book has a simple dedication 'For Elsi' – the poet's wife, the artist Mildred Eldridge. It
is the only book she provides a dust-jacket design for. The dustwrapper blurb reads:
'We publish this first volume by Mr. Thomas in the belief that it will take a permanent
place in our literature.' The copy inscribed by R.S. to his parents is currently for sale
with Gekoski Rare Books in London: 'To my mother and father with love from Ronald.
Christmas 1946.'

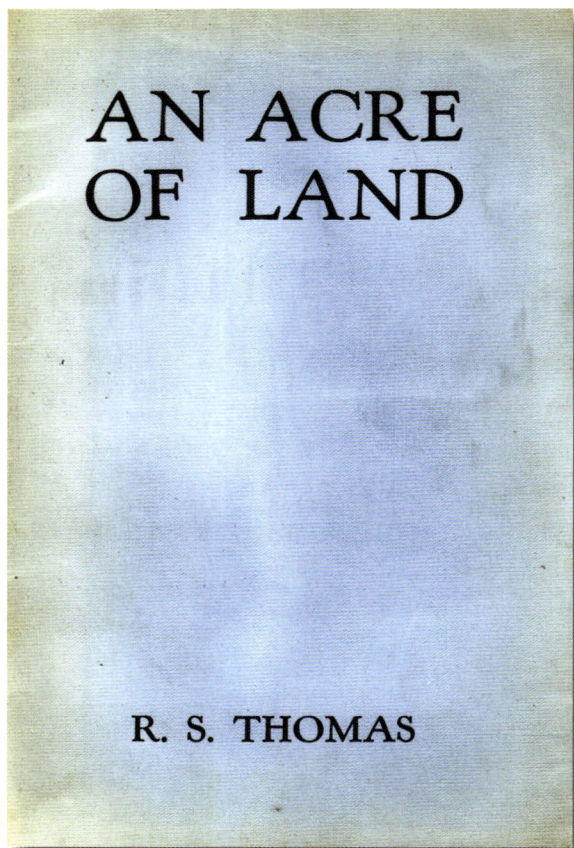

An Acre of Land: Montgomeryshire Printing Co, 1952. Sewn paper covers with a light blue dustjacket vi, 38, 8vo. Another self-published volume, R.S.'s second collection received a sales boost from having been praised on BBC radio by Alan Pryce-Jones, which led to its first edition selling out quickly. It remains perhaps a scarcer proposition than his first collection on account of this spike. Again the publication was financed by the author. The book was issued in a second and third impression and all editions are now elusive.

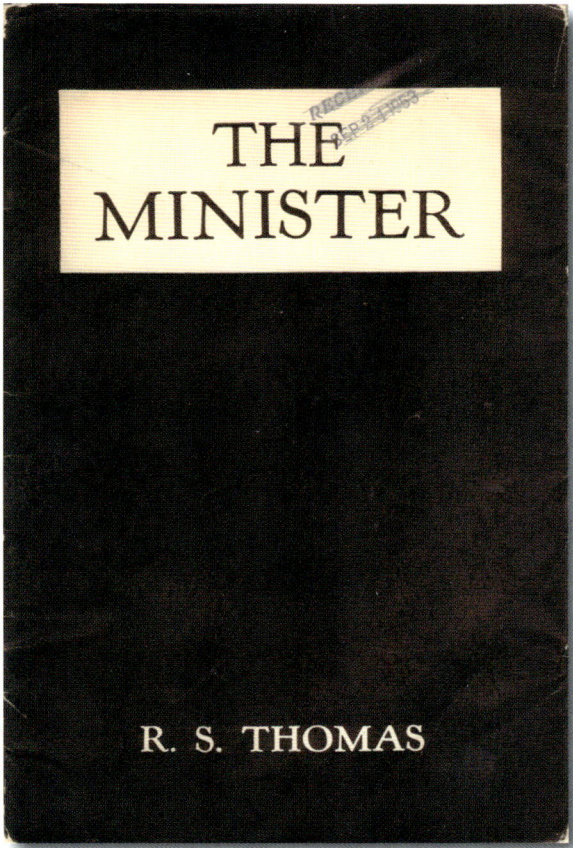

The Minister: The Montgomeryshire Printing Co., Newtown, Montgomeryshire, 1953. Stiff white wrappers with a black dustwrapper. As with his first two publications, R.S. also financed the publication of *The Minister*, which had been commissioned by the BBC for radio broadcast. It was the last time he would resort to such measures. Soon after its publication he told the poet Raymond Garlick: 'I am so hard up that I have almost ceased buying books. I hope the necessity for publishing my own stuff is over.' The copy illustrated came from America and has a small American ownership label pasted inside. The stamped date on the cover suggests it might have been sent to secure U.S. copyright.

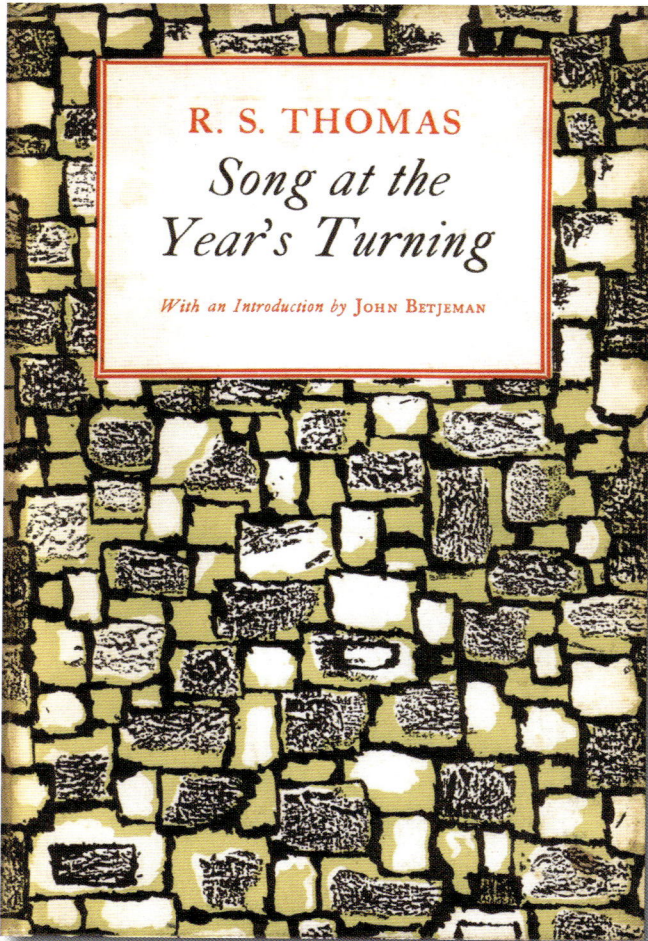

Song at the Year's Turning – Poems 1942-1954: Rupert Hart-Davis, London. 1955. 8vo.115 pages. The fourth book and the first to be properly published by a London publisher. This is the collection which both put an end to the poet's money worries and would cement Thomas's reputation. Its contents comprise shortened versions of his first two books *The Stones of the Field* and *An Acre of Land* and his third book *The Minister*, which is complete, and 19 new poems. The Introduction is by John Betjeman.

WALES

THE NATIONAL MAGAZINE 22

Emyr Humphreys •	Piecepomb for Vjayday
R. S. Thomas •	Hiraeth : Night & Morning
Sir Idris Bell •	Man (D. Gwenallt Jones)
Leslie Norris •	In Merthyr Now
Rhys Davies •	From My Notebook (III)
John Cowper Powys •	Pair Dadeni *or* The Cauldron of Rebirth
Robert D. McIntyre •	A Nationalist at Westminster
Elisabeth Inglis-Jones •	Hafod and Thomas Johnes
Rhys J. Davies, M.P. •	The Mood of the Americans
Tudor Edwards •	Capel-y-Ffin
H. W. Archer •	What's Right with Wales
Clough Williams-Ellis •	Planning Progress in Wales
Harold M. Watkins •	Four M.P.'s
David Jones •	"Wales" Questionnaire, 1946
J. Oliver Stephens •	Keltic War Gods
Sir R. George Stapledon •	Thirty Years a Welshman
T. Hudson-Williams •	Why not learn Russian?
George Woodcock •	Anarchism and Wales
Oswell Blakeston •	Note on Welsh Follies
John Davenport •	"The Condemned Playground"
Eight Welsh Authors by John, Walters, Huws :: Poems	
Reproductions and Caricatures :: Illustrations	
Four-page Art Inset :: Landscape Photographs	

EDITED BY KEIDRYCH RHYS

Vol. VI, No. 2   JUNE, 1946

THE DRUID PRESS

2/6

Keidrych Rhys's WALES The National Magazine. No. 22 June 1946. This is the second series of the periodical (the first eleven issues came out before the war). R.S. contributes two poems, the second 'Night and Morning' is described as being 'From the Welsh Traditional'.

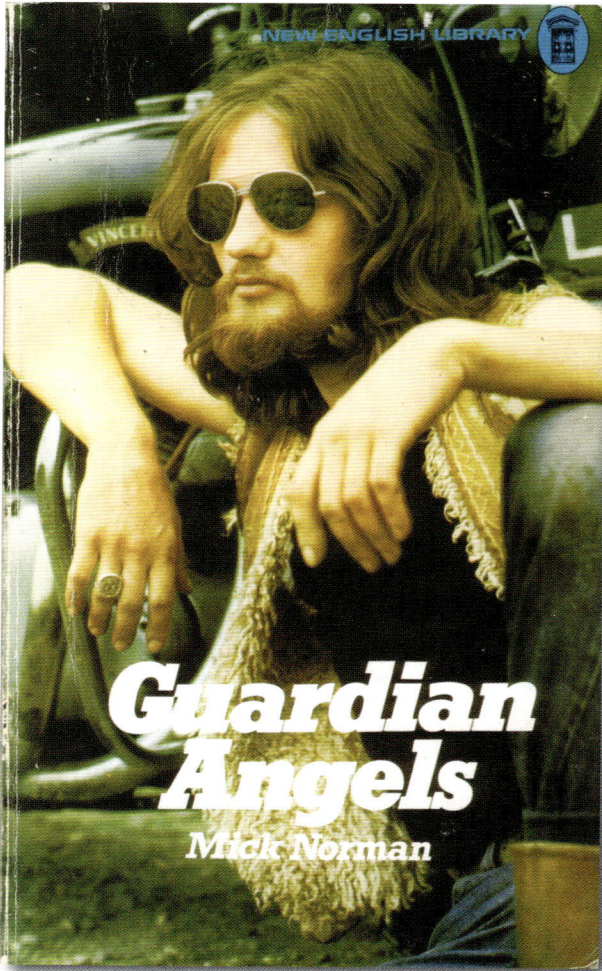

Guardian Angels. *A 1974 generic 'pulp fiction' 'Biker' novel, but curious because page 25 makes surprising literary reference to, 'a local priest and poet from Aberdaron – R.S. Thomas' and goes on to quote eight lines of his poem 'A Welsh Landscape'. Not the usual place one would expect to find R.S. but his poetry addressed a broad church!*

A Welsh-language Periodical; Y FFLAM. Y Nadolig 1946. Contains a prose piece in Welsh by R.S., 'Arian a Swydd', which quotes Yeats (in English). At the end of the issue there is a brief biography of R.S. which references *The Stones of the Field*.

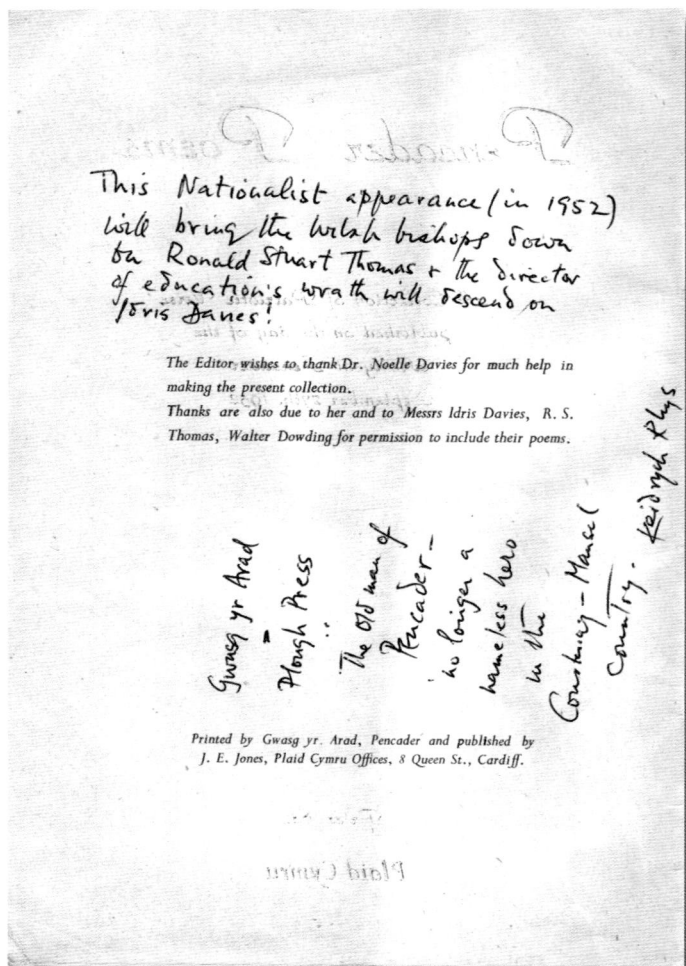

This Nationalist appearance (in 1952)
will bring the Welsh bishops down
on Ronald Stuart Thomas + the Director
of education's wrath will descend on
Idris Davies!

The Editor wishes to thank Dr. Noelle Davies for much help in
making the present collection.
Thanks are also due to her and to Messrs Idris Davies, R. S.
Thomas, Walter Dowding for permission to include their poems.

Gwasg yr Arad

Plough Press

The old man of Pencader — no longer a nameless hero in the

Courtenay — Mance (Country. Keidrych Rhys

Printed by Gwasg yr. Arad, Pencader and published by
J. E. Jones, Plaid Cymru Offices, 8 Queen St., Cardiff.

Pencader Poems. A collection of patriotic verse published on the day of the rally at
Pencader September 27th 1952. A rare Plaid Cymru commemorative pamphlet. Con-
tains R.S.'s poem, 'The Tree'. This copy has been inscribed mischievously by Keidrych
Rhys, 'This Nationalist appearance (in 1952) will bring the Welsh bishops down on
Ronald Stuart Thomas + the director of education's wrath will descend on Idris Davies.'

A Scottish Perspective

Alex Salmond

I wrote a thesis on R.S. Thomas while taking Sixth Year Studies in English at Linlithgow Academy. My teacher suggested R.S. Thomas to me as a poet I would like. Before starting the thesis I wrote to Thomas asking a range of questions about his poems and was surprised and delighted with the very full and meticulous response I got from him. Being able to quote directly from Thomas was, I believe, a major reason why the thesis got an A.

Until that point I had studied the standard English writers to whom you are introduced in secondary schools, including Shakespeare, Wordsworth and Keats and the like. I found Thomas stronger and more meaningful in his writing. His commentaries on political and nationalist issues were particularly interesting.

Regrettably, I never met R.S. Thomas and my only contact was the two wonderful letters he wrote while I was studying for my thesis. However, his widow kindly sent me a CD, shortly after he died, of him reading his poems and I have listened to this many times. I have quoted him on many occasions when his writing has been relevant to a point I have been trying to make.

Thomas's essay on 'Some Contemporary Scottish Writing' (1946) and the essay on 'A Welsh View of the Scottish Renaissance' (1948) were written following a visit to the Hebrides early on in his career. The first essay in particular had a profound effect on making me aware of the quality of contemporary Scottish culture and creativity, much of which at this time was not brought to the fore as it should have been. His second essay led me to consider the connection which Scotland has with Wales and Plaid Cymru.

R.S. Thomas was deeply passionate in his writing and, as his friends attested, he was also very humorous. Strangely, my favourite poem is not a political or social statement but the very simple, yet stirring, 'Song for Gwydion'.

A Rare Bird

Jon Gower

A strange thing happened at one of the memorial events for R.S. Thomas, when he seemed to turn up in the form of a bird. It was a suitably eccentric setting for just such a visitation. We were in the great hall at Portmeirion, that Italianate confection of a village dreamt up by Clough Williams-Elis on the banks of the river Dwyfor. There is always something a little otherworldly about the place, with its magpie architecture, its cobbled piazzas, campaniles and Florentine domes. It was thus a good backdrop for a birding priest to seemingly resurrect in a beating flurry of small feathers.

The baroque village offered a complete contrast and counterpoint to the spare lines of Thomas's poetry being read aloud by his friend and fellow CND activist Menna Elfyn. Then. Then she was interrupted by an insistent tapping sound at the window, which simply refused to stop. It turned out to be a blue tit – and before you suggest anything pragmatic – it wasn't a case of a blue tit dining on the linseed oil in the putty , or eating those tiny red mites which abound in old windowsills. This bird, this acrobatic little passerine, was tapping on the glass, saying 'observe me, I am here'.

It would not have been that surprising that R.S. Thomas had somehow actually inhabited the body of that tiny bird. To begin with, he was a hyper-keen and very able birdwatcher, who could train an eagle eye on the world and, to boot, could tell you exactly what sort of eagle it was – short-toed, Bonelli's or sea eagle. Bird references abound in his poetry, a veritable avifauna. Also in his verse there are other, make-believe or mythical species flying through, as he often invoked the mythological birds of Rhiannon, which could magic the living to sleep or raise the Celtic dead, or Cilgwri's ousel, sounding the silver anvils of their song. In some of his most tender love lyrics, too, Thomas turns to birds for inspiration, such as 'A Marriage' which says how he met his first wife, Mildred Elsi seemingly under a shower of bird-notes and described her bird-like grace.

And then, by way of justifying this mysterious Portmeirion event, this unexpected appearance, there was his own theology, being himself, and in his own words, 'an agnostic when it came to afterlife'. So it would not have surprised me one bit had he flown down from Heaven, or up from the Celtic otherworld, Annwn, or wherever his soul went. For Nature absorbed him, seemed to both heal and sustain him, it was a deep and complete part of him, including his personal theology. In his later years he suggested that 'the Deity has chosen to reveal himself to me via the world of nature'. It might have been present in the warmth felt in a hare's course after the animal itself had scampered away. Or in a country moment, of something glimpsed, intuited even. So maybe it wasn't R.S. at the window after all. Maybe it was God tapping her fingers. Making us alert to the moment.

I really only knew R.S. as a fellow birdwatcher and despite my knowing a little bit about poetry, we hardly ever talked about it. I did, however have the good fortune to take a tape recorder with me when we went out birdwatching and made some radio programmes with the material, and, indeed, this essay. Once I asked him when he first started birdwatching? 'When I wanted to get married I was a curate in Chirk where the vicar didn't want a married curate so I had to move out of the parish to a place out on the Cheshire border, about fifteen miles from the Welsh hills, where there was nothing to do really so I started to take a keen interest in birds. I tried not to neglect my duties but they weren't very rigorous in a country parish. There was no point in visiting country folk by day, as they'd be out in the fields, so I would study in the mornings and go for birdwatching walks in the afternoons.'

Our first meeting was in 1976 when, as a callow youth, I was on my way to take up a job as a voluntary assistant warden on Bardsey for the summer. My parents had driven us up from Llanelli in south Wales but when we got to the cove where the boat was due to leave we found the weather wasn't sufficiently clement for it to get over to the mainland. An inky sky and enormous catspaws capping the waves offshore did not augur well: a lobsterman, busy with his pots tut-tutted his own grim opinion about the likelihood of the boat's coming over.

As my parents and I pondered our next move a tall, rangy man, with a Gorgon flail of grey hair came striding down the path, a pair of industrial-looking binoculars draped around his neck. He may have been wearing a duffle coat, or that may just be memory's tricks, because I later saw that duffle coat a fair bit before he upgraded to an oiled Barbour which he wore into raggedness.

Meeting him there at Porth Meudwy was doubly appropriate. The name means 'hermit's cove' and in a poem called 'Sea-watching' the poet ponders the twin meditations of sea-watching (scanning the waves for rare birds, sometimes for hours) and the business of prayer, the poet himself cast as a hermit.

Porth Meudwy was thus a place entirely suitable to meet R.S., this sometimes solitary mystic, appropriately described by M. Wynn Thomas as 'the laureate of modern loneliness'. The records show that this hermitic cove was also the place where the keen eyed R.S. found his rarest bird. It was not, in fact, a seabird, but rather a red-eyed vireo, a tiny land bird about the size of a parson's thumb, storm-tossed at the tail end of the hurricane season right across the Atlantic. Here, at Porth Meudwy Thomas would spend many a long and meditative hour watching birds.

We chatted in Welsh, although in two very dissimilar dialects, while his dog collar (not the trademark red tie) was enough to persuade my parents to take up his offer of putting me up until the boat came. I well remember one conversation, over a basic supper of bread and cheese, in which we were, for once discussing poetry. I was full of the arrogance of someone who reasonably expected to receive an A grade in my English Literature O-Level. At some point I mentioned Wordsworth and patronisingly informed him 'That Wordsworth was a pantheist poet: do you know what that means?' The idea of asking one of the great pantheist poets of the twentieth century such a dumbass question still makes me squirm.

I was there for almost a week before the weather calmed sufficiently. There were simple suppers of bread and cheese and Cesar Franck on the record player. I seem to recall an image like a Dutch still life of a candle burning in a white shell of a sheep's skull, but that may be memory's fancy.

I think the next time we met was a year or so later when R.S. (as he'd now become to me in letters) was addressing the Dylan Thomas Summer School at Swansea University. The venue was conveniently near to Blackpill, the sandy sweep of shoreline that stretches between Swansea and Oystermouth, where a very rare bird indeed had recently been sighted, namely a ring-billed gull, an ocean's breadth away from its usual coastal habitats in America. I took him along to scan through the flocks of herring gulls and lesser black-backs and luckily we spotted the tell-tale ring around one bird's bill. While he was down south we also went to look for one of the very first pairs of goshawk nesting in Wales, deep among the sitka ranks of Pembrey forest and again luck was on our side, and we saw both the ferocious looking female on the nest and the male coming back, fresh from hunting crows and squirrels.

After that we would meet occasionally and we grew to have naturalist friends in common, not least *The Guardian* Country Diarist William, or Bill, Condry. Condry was one of the most quiet and unassuming men you could ever meet, the sort who would spot an adder slowly waking up in the spring sunshine and quietly caress the serpent's head. Little wonder that he and his wife Penny once had a pair of wild birds nesting in their bedroom, so quiet and respectful of nature were they. R.S. and Bill shared a love of silence as well as birdsong.

Bill Condry was responsible for R.S. moving to the edge of the Dyfi estuary, and together they campaigned for establishment of the RSPB's Ynys-hir reserve, which Bill later wardened. The vicar of Eglwys-fach had retired and Condry, knowing of R.S.'s interest in the west side of Wales, wrote to him, suggesting he applied for the job. It was a great success from Condry's point of view because not only did the church manage to fill the position but he got a fellow birdwatcher into the bargain: 'I was very impressed by this chap because he was so earnest about his birds and took them so seriously and I thought here we are, we've got a traditional parson naturalist here in the good old Gilbert White of Selbourne tradition, so I was terribly taken with R.S.' One imagines that White, with his patient detailing of the year's subtle changes in his Hampshire parish would indeed have found a soul-mate in R.S.

In addition to the winter flock of Greenland white-fronted geese and wheeling flocks of wigeon, here at Eglwys-fach R.S. encountered various versions of the human species, including many English settlers, with a good few from a military background. He upset one or three when he painted the church pews pitch black with the artistic input of wife Elsi. Considering his sometimes dour outlook on life it might have been his way of brightening the place up a bit because he could be a bit of a misanthrope! As he has observed:

I've had more pleasure from being alone with the natural creation than I have with human beings. Human beings are responsible for so much unhappiness and cruelty and failure that one is not terribly enthusiastic about them.

But that sometimes bitter take on humanity did not mean he was not a good custodian of his flock. The former Archbishop of Canterbury, Rowan Williams, thinks he could be a very good priest as well as a gifted poet:

A photo which was taken by the 20th century monk and spiritual writer Thomas Merton shows a large iron hook hanging against an empty sky – it looks like a meat hook, but it also looks like a question mark and Merton captioned it, 'The only known photograph of God'. I think R.S. would have responded to that. This is not a poetry that seeks to gloss or explain or communicate a set of religious ideas. It's pushing you all the time, saying if this word is in our vocabulary, what's it there for? Clearly for those he knew needed him he could be a brilliant pastor, no two ways about that, but that's pretty rare. I guess for the most part he would have said I'm here to do the ritual things, I'm here to be a reminder to this rural community, whether they like it or not, of that great meat hook hanging from the sky. (He was) there for the sake of that sheer, inescapable, metaphysical awkwardness, as in the Old Testament, in Ezekiel, whether they hear or refuse to hear...

At Eglwys-fach, which, appropriately enough, means little church, R.S. and Bill Condry would spend many a pleasant (and presumably quiet) day together wandering the bird-filled marshes or ranging the Ceredigion hills, even, occasionally, venturing into Europe in search of birds. Once, on a Continental adventure they were in France where they spotted a Montagu's harrier. They stopped the car to train their binoculars on this elegant bird of prey. The next thing the French Air Force police turned up to arrest them for allegedly spying on the air base, detaining the two for a day and interrogating them. They asked R.S. about his career as a clergyman and, at one point he mentioned his son Gwydion. The French cops, used to Catholic priests, who were childless, thought they'd tripped him up. It took some explaining. Eventually, released from custody, R.S. and Bill spent an amiable month in France and Spain, accruing quite a list of birds. After he retired R.S. would go on birding holidays, in Poland or on the Scilly Isles, including one holiday in Greece where he climbed Mount Olympus and instead of encountering God found a crested tit!

Bill Condry would recall how R.S. was a very funny man, an opinion shared by other friends of his, such as fellow poet and bird-enthusiast Gwyneth Lewis, who can recall many a side-splitting moment when they went together to read their work in Barcelona. Lewis once asked him how he got from one poetic line to another and he answered that he put two lines together and waited for them to breed.

R.S. Thomas *was* funny, and a good bird mimic who could do a cracking shelduck impression up there with Percy Thrower. I remember visiting the tern colony with him at Cemlyn Lagoon where he could *kirrick* with the best of the sandwich terns: truly there was a bit of the Doolittle about him.

He also looked a bit like a bird, as Byron Rogers, author of the more readable of the two R.S. biographies avers. Rogers remembers the first time they met:

> *I've never seen a man look more like a poet – this hawk face, this wintry smile.*

Thomas had arranged to meet Rogers for tea in one of the seafront hotels in Aberystwyth:

> *He was always very proper was Ronald. I was seventeen: I hero worshipped this man, and there were many, many vicars going by on the front at Aberystwyth. One was a fat one, one was a chap with specs, but then a third one came...with this hawk face...*

Describing R.S. as possessed of accipitrine features would be a relief to Rowan Williams, who can't abide the clichéd ways of describing RS:

> *There are many recurring ways of describing R.S. His features are often described as craggy. The battle with the clichés about him is often lost: if I see the word 'craggy' one more time I shall scream.*

When I visited Rowan Williams, he was just moving into the Master's Lodge at Magdalene College, Cambridge and my eye was immediately drawn to the prominent shelf full of R.S. Thomas's books. Williams, who is, of course, also a fine poet, admires the way in which Thomas pares things back to the bone, so that the language is often stark, spare and unadorned such as, in 'The Parish' with its imagery of sharp beaks tearing prey.

'Birds and man are so often interlinked and intertwined in Thomas's work,' former National Poet of Wales Gwyneth Lewis suggests of this poem, 'You can never see a bird on its own, it's always a bird combined with a person and that's the great strand of his nature poetry for me.' After R.S.'s death Gwyneth was given a copy of one of R.S.'s books, P.A.D. Hollom's *Popular Handbook of British Birds* by his widow Betty. The real treasure, perhaps, was tucked inside, being the British Trust for Ornithology's *Checklist of British Birds*, with a tick next to each of the species R.S. had ever seen, thus his life-list of birds, including the red-eyed vireo, which had to be written in by hand. Of course a life list, over time, becomes a list of all the birds you *haven't* seen, of those you will not have enough time to see. As time itself migrates, flies away from you.

One of Lewis's favourite R.S. bird poems is 'The Place' in which the returning, migratory house martins literally inhabit the poet, after returning from their migrations.

For Gwyneth Lewis this melding of man and martin, of man into nature and nature in man, touches 'the very greatness of his insight into birds'. The former Poet Laureate Andrew Motion concurs with this opinion:

> *I've always thought that there were two categories of people who write about nature in general, and birds in particular. There are those that by showing tremendous sympathy and empathy with the activities of natural things they can some-how melt into them, and you can say that of Ted Hughes and that at least part of the dynamism of his language is to say 'look at me, I'm a bird too', or like Gerard Manley Hopkins when he says 'I am the windhover'. Then there are other poets who say that what they find fascinating about birds is that we are really not like them, and I see almost all R.S. Thomas's poems being positioned around that question. There's a part of him that wants to be a bird, wants that free-dom, wants to be exonerated of the foolishness and the frenzy of humanity but he can't do it and he can't do it partly be-cause he's conscious of their otherness and partly, I think, for moral reasons, the feeling it would be an escape, he can't let himself.*

Nature, though – as William Blake has famously pointed out – is not always benign, but is, rather, red in tooth and claw. It's the sort of nature very evident in one of Rowan Williams's favourite R.S. Thomas poems, 'The Raptor', where the natural world generates some of Thomas's most painfully ambivalent images, of cruelty and waste and caprice:

There's a sense when R.S. writes of God as a bird of prey...
he's talking about his own consciousness, but it's interesting
that at the end of that poem the raptor screams as he buries
his talons in the adversary, or not God's enemy, the devil,
whatever, in evil, or sin but in us as if God can't tell the dif-
ference between friend and enemy but just grabs.

I have a lurking suspicion that as Thomas peregrinated from one parish to the next it was usually to one where he could grab better birding. Certainly the last of his parishes, St Hywyn's in Aberdaron, on the wind-flailed Llŷn peninsula was a great place for birding: once a rare shrike settled briefly in the churchyard, attracting scores of ornithologists to scope among the headstones. And of course, just offshore was the end of an old spiritual highway and Ynys Enlli, burial place of 20,000 saints or pilgrims.

This was a perfect parish for Thomas, a life-long lover of the sea, whose father had been a sea captain. He envisaged Llŷn as a bough suspended between sea and sky, a liminal place, a strange, enchanted land, with shearwaters offshore. So, choosing to come to this westernmost, Welsh-speaking parish was easy, what with the extra attraction of the best bird-watching of any of his church postings. One day I had the temerity to suggest that this was the case. He fixed me with a gimlet eye – the eye of a Bonelli's eagle perhaps – and suggested that I was on dangerous ground. He almost grinned as he said it. Almost:

You're on dangerous ground, now. Ha! The thing is in Wales
people preferred to be in busier places, in towns and so on,
so I didn't feel particularly guilty about wanting to go to
wilder parishes. I had to do my duties but I was certainly
lucky...

Here, in Aberdaron, at land's end, this Welsh Finistère, he could fully be the hermit of the rocks, waiting simply, sea-watching, sentient and ultra-alert for that rare bird, which sometimes had already flown by. A pomarine skua. A sooty shearwater. God. That albino dunnock.

As Rowan Williams points out, this is fully a part of the Christian mystical tradition:

> *You look round at the world and you see something that's just passed you. Everything in the world seems to just point to say he (or He) went that way. I think a little bit of that gets into R.S., the sense there's something enormous just out of view. And the sea, that has a lot to do both with God and with human identity, and human love and human emotion which are very present in the later collections.*

R.S. could find solace and beauty in birds, their songs, their flights, their unexpected appearances. For him the ritual of birdwatching was a sort of meditation, of prayer and, too, a celebration, of the world's extraordinary patterning. What he observed in marsh and on mountain, on sculpted shore and rocky headland, allowed shafts of optimism to break, like sunlight through glowering skies because, in his words 'I suppose I have been chosen, along with other people to receive a revelation via nature. I feel more able to be religious and to worship in the countryside than in the town... The beauty of the world, the created earth is so beautiful – trees birds clouds – you can't be a complete pessimist with so much beauty around.'

It's an epiphanic beauty that radiates – simply, steadily and truthfully – from so much of R.S.'s work, as he allows language to get airborne, takes ideas constantly aloft, throws carefully chosen words like showers or sprays of birds into the clear, sustaining and surrounding air. They fly at you, roost in you, get their claws into you. Words, birds, that both rhyme and chime. His legacy. His illuminations.

Remembering the Peacemaker

Menna Elfyn

I have always envied poets who share a kind of camaraderie. One fine example is Cylch Cadwgan, the Cadwgan Circle, in south Wales, a group of erudite poets and intellectuals that included Pennar Davies, J. Gwyn Griffiths, Kate Bosse-Griffiths, and Rhydwen Williams, who were socially and politically active and alert to the importance of poetry as they strove to create new possibilities for writing in Welsh.

Such a fellowship, alien to me, would also have been alien to the kind of poet R.S. Thomas was to become. He belonged to that other kind of poet who demands distance and a sense of solitude, a self-imposed exile almost. 'Guard your solitude,' Rilke warned, and R.S. did indeed guard his solitude which was a world away from the close fellowship of Cylch Cadwgan. And it's with this inward-dialogue with the self that I identified most readily in R.S., when absorbing his work. Later, we both understood that discussing mundane subjects with one another was a subterfuge, in case we strayed into that very private domain. The private life of the writer seemed even more necessary for someone whose calling as a priest meant endless services, tea parties, baptisms, weddings, and funerals.

I grew to understand a little of R.S. Thomas's psyche in that I too grew up in the Manse and learned that an early morning telephone call meant death, the shy couple at the door a wedding to be arranged. As the minister's children, we soon learned to disappear to our bedrooms whenever a member of the chapel called, wanting to be out of the way. This is perhaps what R.S. also wanted more than anything – to be out of the way in solitude. The tedium of being a minister is well articulated in his poem *The Minister*, but I am sometimes puzzled as to why he didn't become a chapel minister himself – where there would have been a degree of independence from the rigid hierarchy of Church, Queen and State. Yet it is understandable that he sought his livelihood in the Church in Wales as his sense of Welsh identity wasn't fully formed when he took holy orders. One could argue that he came to know his parishioners far better than if he had become a Nonconformist minister, as the priest was meant to represent the whole parish and not just one section of the community.

It can also be said that the difference between the minister and vicar's vocation is relatively small. In every parish, there will be those who will want to obtain favour, become his closest friend, but the minister who is wise will keep a degree of detachment. And therein lies the contradiction, for there is no one who gets closer to a family than a person who has to console and bear witness to people at the end of their lives. He is, as David Jones quipped on another issue, 'something of a vicar whose job is legatine – a kind of *servus servorum*'. R.S. Thomas seems to me to be the mirror image of his contemporary, the Trappist monk Thomas Merton, who also embraced the Welsh side of his heritage. Both seemed ill-equipped to live as they did, Merton in the hermitage in Gethsemani, and R.S. in Aberdaron; each a solitary in his own way but also needing some kind of dialogue and connection with people. Merton admits in *Thoughts on Silence*:

> *Contradictions have always existed in the soul of man. But it is only when we prefer analysis to silence that they become a constant and insoluble problem. We are not meant to re-solve all contradictions but to live with them and rise above them and see them in the light of exterior and objective val-ues which make them trivial by comparison.*

And in another passage he maintained that silence belonged to the substance of sanctity asserting that 'when we have really met and known the world in silence, words do not separate us from the world nor from other men, nor from God.'

Another contradiction in the public held image of R.S. is that he loved Kierkegaard who was regarded by many as the funniest philosopher of all time. Søren Kierkegaard's writings, according to Thomas C. Oden, revel in a comedy of contradictions that are inherent in the human condition as he dispels the notion of him as a philosopher of despair. One could also say of R.S. that he was an Either/Or figure in many of his strongly held opinions – which were often caricatured in the press. In this respect, Kierkegaard has a wonderful illustration:

> *The relation between the daily press and authors is as follows. An author writes a coherent and consistently clear presentation of some idea – perhaps even the fruit of many years of labour. No one reads it. But a journalist, in reviewing the book takes the occasion to slap together some rubbish which he presents as representing the author's book – this everyone reads. We see the author's significance in existence – he exists so that a journalist can have the occasion to write some rubbish which everyone reads.*

R.S. was certainly misrepresented in various newspaper articles. He was also portrayed unfairly in visual terms, the nadir being a television programme which showed him preaching to an empty church.

R.S. was also passionate about safeguarding the future of the Welsh language and its culture, and felt compelled to express these views strongly on this subject. He was instrumental in founding Cyfeillion Llŷn, The Friends of Llŷn, a society to support the Welsh-language culture of the Llŷn Peninsula. He wrote to ask me whether we could meet at the Eisteddfod for tea as he wanted to discuss the possibility of setting up Cyfeillion Ceredigion along the same lines as that of Cyfeillion Llŷn. Yet he found me an unwilling accomplice. I wrote back to say that I felt that Wales had far too many societies. Perhaps I was wrong to dismiss his wish outright and should have at least listened to his argument. If I'm honest, I'd say that I felt queasy at the thought of having to organise a society, let alone belong to one. Belonging is another difficult word in a poet's lexicon. And here I return to the idea of solitude – of defending it – remembering his essay 'Hunan Laddiad y Llenor' (The Suicide of the Writer), where he argued that to be a poet in Wales one had to succumb to participating in so many causes and events.

I am at times, disappointed at myself for dismissing his plan. How could I not have granted his wish? I admired him for his total commitment to poetry but also his passion for Wales and the Welsh language. He translated two of my poems into English, 'Song of a Voiceless Person to BT', in the early Nineties. In a letter, he berated me for wanting to translate my work but at the tail end of the letter just under his signature 'R.S.' were the words, '*wedi gwneud fy ngorau*' (I've tried my best). On the other side of the letter was a magnificent translation. Later, he translated another poem of mine for my first bilingual poetry collection, *Eucalyptus* (Gomer, 1995), and wrote a glowing blurb for the second edition of the same book. However, we never discussed the issue of translation again as he felt disappointed at a response to his translations. And I never asked him again.

People also forget that he was a campaigner for peace, and again the comparison with Thomas Merton is interesting. He would drive long distances to get to marches and protests which were only attended by around a hundred people. Even in these gatherings, he seemed to be 'elsewhere' or chiding the apathy of the Welsh. '*Sdim llawer yma*' (Not many here), would be his constant refrain to me. But if at times, he seemed to have been 'elsewhere', he also knew how to 'return to the world', to be in the here and now as well as recognising the necessity of challenging the existing order. I conclude by recalling such an occasion at an anti-nuclear rally in Carmarthen. He came and marched, listening intently before leaving quietly with only a hand raised to acknowledge to me that he was off. I, like many feel blessed in following his way of living through poetry, which he describes as 'that which arrives at the intellect by way of the heart'. That seems a perfect synthesis of all the contradictions inherent in R.S. and his poetry; but it also reveals the life of a visionary, one who lived and worked to make poetry both urgent and timeless.

Peacemaker

(in memory of R.S. Thomas at a protest march in the late '80s)

You died at least once before:
that afternoon on Nott Square
when you were a ghost for peace.
Arms and legs making frost angels
of the frozen floor beneath you.
You whispered, 'we're thin on the ground'
and I heard that tetch in your voice,
chiding, yet loving your neighbour.

And when it thawed we rose again
obeying the celestial claxon call
announcing a good day's work for peace.
But I knew well enough as you waved me farewell
– now it is time to leave for home –
that the world outside would be unkind,
with its rind of rime on the road.

Us? We lingered a while,
freezing, by Ferrar's tombstone,
that martyr who knew
the meaning of unshakeable:

For me, you had kidnapped a day
on the eve of the Sabbath, driving
the twisting road from the north
to bear witness with a motley crew
stretched longshanks on concrete.

Yet this is the poet's true, silent protest: withdrawal,
turning in on the self, losing, losing
this world for a while.

And for the blink of an eye
there you were, your wordless banner raised
high above the clouds of witnesses.

Menna Elfyn
(Translated from the Welsh by Elin ap Hywel)

In the Chapel of the Spirit

Grahame Davies

I first came across R.S. Thomas's name on a poster of his poem 'Cynddylan on a Tractor'. The image of flat-capped Cynddylan steering his red, retro machine towards the viewer was displayed on the wall of the English class in Ysgol Morgan Llwyd, the Welsh-medium comprehensive school which I attended in the town of Wrexham in north-east Wales in the late 1970s.

The image was set above the window that looked west towards my home, Coedpoeth, a former coal-mining village piled against a hillside below the brown bulk of the Berwyn Mountains. Behind that high, heather-covered rampart was, I suspected, a Wales more rural, more mysterious, more unchanged, and certainly more Welsh than the industrial borderland where we lived, on that exposed eastward-facing slope between the hills and the English plain. At that time, longing to escape from lessons in order to wander the countryside around my home village, I can't say I understood the full implications of the poet's reference to 'the machine': symbolic critiques of industrial materialism were beyond me at that age. But the desire for something more rooted, more primal, more real, yes, I think I understood that. I understood too, that if you wanted it, you had to look west.

Perhaps that's why I have always had such a strong regard for R.S. Thomas. After all, some thirty years previously, a young man in his thirties, he had looked in precisely the same direction. During the Second World War, he was a curate at Hanmer, a few miles east of Wrexham and close to the English border. One night, in August 1940, he watched a bombing raid turn that same Berwyn Mountain to flame. German aircraft, mistaking the chimneys of the area's lead mines for industrial sites on blacked-out Merseyside, had bombed the district for two successive nights. The light of that conflagration provided the young pacifist priest with unexpected illumination: this industrial-scale destruction was a product of the machine age; he would escape it, he would go back to the land, back to the old ways and the old language, back to the west, where it was the setting sun, not war machines, that turned the mountains to fire.

By the time I came across his work, R.S. was in his sixties, his journey back to the wild Welsh west complete: he was the priest of Aberdaron, at the furthest tip of the Llŷn peninsula; he had long been fluent in Welsh; he was the most outspoken advocate of radical Welsh nationalism; the most prominent Welsh poet of his generation. The furthest, the most famous, most fiery, most forbidding. He had become a figure to whom superlatives were drawn like gulls to a sea stack. His isolation had brought stature; his reticence, respect; he had withdrawn into pre-eminence.

I met him first in 1980, by which time I was studying English in Yale Sixth Form College in Wrexham, the shock of my emergence from my previous Welsh-speaking enclave having newly sensitised me to the value of the culture which I had hitherto taken for granted, and having given me a new appreciation of what Thomas was saying. R.S. was doing a reading at Wrexham's Library, and I managed to catch a few words with him afterwards. The content of that exchange was of little substance, but great consequence, because, a year later, as I was being interviewed for a place at what is now Anglia Ruskin University in Cambridge, an account of that meeting with Thomas, and an ensuing exploration of the cultural position he represented, provided the main material of the discussion, arming me with sudden, invaluable expertise. The interviewer was a huge fan of Thomas and had never before had the chance to discuss his work with a real live Welsh-speaker, fresh from the hills; I was offered a place to study English Literature. It could hardly have been further from the mountains of the west, but exiles carry their landscape within them, so I wrote my dissertation on R.S. Thomas, corresponding with him tentatively in the process. Over the years that followed, as I published some reviews and articles, I found myself a member of that then small, now numerous, group of writers and commentators for whom the primary material of R.S. Thomas's lifelong struggle with the elemental questions of existence provided endless substance for our secondary speculations. Like the birds following

Cynddylan's tractor, we sought our sustenance in his wake.

A few years after graduating and then training as a journalist, I found myself encountering R.S. Thomas in a very different context. In my then job as a newspaper reporter, in the early 1990s, at a time of unrest in sections of the nationalist community, I was sent to cover the meeting of a radical group who had, controversially, been linked to support for violence. R.S. Thomas was due to speak at their meeting in Owain Glyndŵr's parliament house in Machynlleth. After his speech, he and I both had to leave the meeting; I because a journalist was no longer welcome during what were now to be secret discussions, and R.S. because he was not formally a member of the group. While the meeting proceeded without us, we sat alone together in the small stone anteroom of what was reputed to be the first Welsh parliament. Never one for small-talk, least of all with a member of the press, Thomas said nothing; I had gathered all I needed for journalistic purposes from his public speech and did not want to mix personal and professional interests by opening a conversation under those strained circumstances. We passed the time in silence, neither journalist nor poet able to find the words.

Shortly afterwards, I decided to pursue doctoral research in the Welsh Department in Cardiff University, taking R.S. Thomas, of course, as my subject. By now, however, I was beginning to take an interest in the ways in which Thomas's standpoint offered a perspective on issues beyond the confines of the internal cultural debates of my own country. I opted to compare him with some other twentieth-century cultural figures who had, it seemed to me, also consciously chosen to identify with particular national communities and who had also become outstanding spokespeople for a particular form of nationalism rooted in tradition, language, and land. The three examples were T.S. Eliot, Saunders Lewis and Simone Weil. Each seemed, within their individual cultures, an exceptional figure: an outsider who had adopted a particular defensive project of national cultural survival as part of a challengingly traditionalist critique of the modern world as experienced in the turbulent years of the early to mid twentieth century. Singular within their own cultures, they nonetheless shared many similarities when viewed together; an alliance of anomalies.

Eliot, born in St Louis, Missouri, in 1888, came to England in his mid twenties and, although he was a daring and radical innovator in his use of poetic form, he soon adopted an arch-conservative cultural position deeply concerned with protecting threatened Englishness, particularly during the Second World War, the background to his mature masterpiece, *Four Quartets*. Saunders Lewis was born five years later, and although brought up in the Welsh-speaking community of Liverpool, he went to an English public school and did not come to Wales to live until his late twenties. One of the founders of Welsh political nationalism, he too adopted a conservative political position, deeply influenced by the same Catholic social teaching that had informed the thought of the Anglo-Catholic convert Eliot, of whom Lewis, himself a convert to Catholicism, was an admirer. Simone Weil, born in 1909, and brought up by liberal Jewish parents, was a lifelong activist on the radical left; under the pressure of Nazi occupation of her homeland, she became first an internal refugee and then an exile, and, in the last years of her brief life (she died in 1943), formed an inspiring vision of the importance of the national community rooted in tradition, the land and the Catholic faith to which she almost, but not quite, converted. All three had a tendency to religious mysticism, all three met the challenge of the modern world by promoting a vision of rooted, religious, culturally integrative, traditionalist national communities. Taken together, they could be seen as part of a pattern across Europe in which deracinated intellectuals sought, by adopting particular national movements, to choose a ground for their opposition to what they saw as the destructive effects of an increasingly mechanised, massified, urbanised and materialist society. Viewed in their company, R.S. Thomas seemed less an isolated glacial erratic, more an outcrop of a particular flinty substratum running through European culture.

That wider context, I believe, added to his status. For many readers, critics and commentators it seemed that Thomas was defined primarily by his position with respect to the specific current politics of Wales itself, and was to be praised or dismissed according to the observer's degree of sympathy with that viewpoint. However, this could be said to be too restrictive a view. The matter of Wales is not the main subject of Thomas's work, and in terms of his hierarchy of values, it seems explicitly subordinate to his wider concerns about modernity and materialism. Wales was where he chose to make his stand, certainly, but his campaign was against what he saw as a global threat. Like Eliot, Lewis, Weil and others, he joined a national struggle in pursuit of an international objective – the preservation of a spiritual world view, and the human values flowing from that, in the face of what seemed like soulless reductivism. Materialism, the 'Machine', not England, was the adversary.

Over the years that followed, I had the opportunity to test this thesis with R.S. Thomas on several occasions. My first serious conversation was in November 1992 when R.S. agreed to be interviewed to help me with my research. We met at his cottage at Sarn Rhiw in Pen Llŷn. The first sight which greeted the visitor on stooping to enter the dark interior of that forbidding stone building was a sheep's skull placed on a wooden chest directly opposite the entrance; standing next to it was a plain Christian cross. Not quite the skull and crossbones, but not far off. It was, I came to realise, part of the almost theatrical paraphernalia of seclusion with which R.S., in some ways a very public recluse, surrounded himself in order to guard the solitude from which he knew his work arose. As R.S.'s many friends can testify – that very phrase gives the lie to the reclusive image – the real man could be warmer, kinder and funnier than the stone-faced soothsayer he was often perceived as being. On the day that we met, the television-less Thomas had arranged the timing of our interview so that he would be free in the afternoon to watch the Wales–Australia rugby international in a friend's house.

We spoke in the kitchen, while winter birds thronged the bush which pressed against the back window. Seeking to find connections between my four authors, I asked Thomas about his first meeting with Saunders Lewis in the summer of 1945. At that time, Thomas had only recently become a convert to Welsh nationalism, and, inspired by one of Lewis's articles, he decided he would go straight to the fountainhead, turning up unannounced at Lewis's home and declaring, in English, that he had come to offer his services to the cause. Welcomed in, and encouraged by Lewis to use his still-halting Welsh, Thomas spoke about his vision for Wales. It was the start of a career which would end, half a century later, with Thomas having, to a considerable extent, adopted the mantle of his hero.

At the time I was conducting my research, academic study on R.S. Thomas was something of a cottage craft: the number of books about Thomas himself was in single figures, and the aspiring scholar could have reasonably expected to read all the author's work and everything else written about him, with comparative ease. My own doctorate was completed in 1997 and the subsequent book, *Sefyll yn y Bwlch*, appeared two years later. Over the ensuing years my path crossed several times with Thomas's as my own academic and literary life became busier, and as his fame increased. A decade or so later, and particularly after the author's death, studies of this apostle of localness had gone global. With an ever-expanding body of research and comment, the studies of those earlier days seemed like some simpler, pre-industrial idyll; Cynddylan before the tractor. By now, diligent scholars have unearthed ever more material; the work and the life are being studied from ever more perspectives, while those viewpoints are themselves then examined and re-examined, tested and contested.

In the poem 'Welsh History', in one of his most memorable images for what he saw as the condition of his country, R.S. Thomas depicts his people in the menial role of having to quarrel for crumbs fallen from the table. Those words might stand too as a caution to those debating a mighty literary legacy. But, leaving aside the suggestion of dispute, the image also clearly recalls the words of the faithful Syro-Phoenician woman in Mark's and Matthew's Gospels, or those of communicants at the mass who declare themselves unworthy to gather up the crumbs under God's table. As such, they call to mind Thomas's relentless orientation towards the possibility of a transcendent spiritual reality, however elusive. This, it seems to me, was the central experience of the poet's existence from the earliest years of his career.

In 1948, Thomas published an article in Welsh entitled '*Dau Gapel*' (Two Chapels) in which he recounts his experience of visiting two upland places of worship, Soar-y-Mynydd in Ceredigion and Maesyronnen in Radnorshire, in search, as he put it, of the soul of the true Welshman. There is certainly some unintended irony in this man who loved his country more than his countrymen searching for the essential soul of a people in the parts of Wales most devoid of human presence. But one must allow Thomas the integrity of his own vision, especially in the light of what his solitary journeys brought him. The remoter Soar-y-Mynydd he says represents the soul, as it displays the communal Welsh experience of resilience and endurance in the face of adversity. Maesyronnen, however, represents the spirit, and does so because of the extraordinary mystical vision Thomas experienced during his visit there, and which he describes in vivid terms, comparing the moment with the revelations of St John on the island of Patmos. Thomas says the experience defied description, but that, in essence, it showed him that time was an illusion and that all existence is the perpetual emanation of an eternal God. He concludes by saying that of the two chapels he must choose that of the soul, as no one can live continually in the spirit. That is undoubtedly, and sadly, true. But it is also true that no one who has ever had such an experience can ever forget it. All one's subsequent life is lived, if not in the light of that experience, then certainly in the shadow cast by that light.

It is that shadow, perhaps, which so often seems to darken with disappointment the poet's view of the natural world, of human relationships, and of society as a whole – even that of the Wales he would most wished to have idealised. But disappointment needs desire, just as shadows need the sun, and few poets can have lived and communicated this creative chiaroscuro as faithfully and attentively as R.S. Thomas.

As part of the poet's centenary celebrations, I was asked, with other writers, to contribute a poem to a tribute event. In responding to that commission, I could not help but be drawn to what seemed to me the most pivotal experience of R.S. Thomas's inner life: that transformative, and ultimately inexpressible mystical vision that makes him one of the greatest religious poets of his age.

CAPEL MAESYRONNEN

Yma y daethost, yn llanc,
â dyn a duw yn ifanc,
i geisio enaid Cymru
ymhell o'i haelwydydd hi,
a chael – er bod drws dan glo
a dim ond gwynt yn groeso,
ac er dy fod dithau'n neb –
agor drws tragwyddoldeb.
A blasu ffynnon ddi-baid
yr un a'r unig enaid,
a chael cyflawnder dy gred
ar fryn yn Sir Maesyfed.
I dithau, wedyn, oes hir
yng nghysgod haul y gweundir.
I ninnau, briwsion mawredd
heb inni erioed flasu'r wledd.

MAESYRONNEN CHAPEL

You came here, a youth,
when God and man were young,
to seek the soul of Wales
far from her firesides,
and you found – though the door was locked
and there was only the wind for welcome,
and though you yourself were no-one –
that the door of eternity stood open.
You tasted the endless fountain
of the only, single soul,
and found your faith's fullness
on a hillside in Maesyfed.
Yours, thereafter, a long life
in the shadow of the moorland sun.
Ours, the crumbs of greatness
who yet had never tasted the feast.

Contributors

Gillian Clarke
Gillian Clarke has been National Poet for Wales since 2008. She is President of Tŷ Newydd, the Welsh Writers Centre, which she co-founded in 1990. Her recent collection of poems, *Ice*, was short-listed for the T.S. Eliot Award 2012. In December 2010 she was awarded the Queen's Gold Medal for Poetry, and in 2012 the Wilfred Owen Award.

Fflur Dafydd
Novelist and screenwriter Fflur Dafydd lectures in Creative Writing at Swansea University. She is the Hay International Fellow 2013-14 and her documentary *Pererindod R.S.* will be broadcast on S4C in December 2013. Her latest fiction title is *The White Trail* (Seren, 2011).

Grahame Davies
Grahame Davies is a poet, novelist, editor and literary critic and a winner of the Wales Book of the Year Award. The author of 17 books in Welsh and English, he has a degree in English from Anglia Ruskin University, Cambridge, a PhD in Welsh from Cardiff University and has been awarded an Hon. DLitt from Anglia Ruskin. A native of Coedpoeth near Wrexham, he has lived for many years in south Wales and now divides his time between Cardiff and London.

Menna Elfyn
Menna Elfyn is an award winning poet and playwright and the author of 13 volumes of poetry. Her most recent collection, *Murmur*, was a Poetry Book Society Recommended Translation in Autumn 2012 and the first ever award for a bilingual Welsh/English volume. She is Director of Creative Writing at the University of Wales, Trinity Saint David.

Peter Finch

Peter Finch is a poet and psychogeographer living in Cardiff. He has published more than thirty books including the series *Real Cardiff*. His poetry appears in *Selected Later Poems* and *Zen Cymru*, both published by Seren. His latest book is *Edging The Estuary – Chepstow to Worm's Head, Gloucester to Lynmouth, The Barrage, the islands and the grey brown water* (Seren, 2013).

Jon Gower

Jon Gower is a writer and broadcaster who has seventeen books to his name: these include *Y Storïwr*, which won the Wales Book of the Year Award in 2012, the coastal journey *Wales: At Water's Edge* which was shortlisted for the 2013 prize, and *The Story of Wales*, which accompanies the landmark BBC television series.

Gwyneth Lewis

Gwyneth Lewis was National Poet of Wales 2005-06. She is an award-winning poet in both Welsh and English and composed the six-foot high words on the front of the Wales Millennium Centre. Her non-fiction books are *Sunbathing in the Rain: A Cheerful Book on Depression* and *Two in a Boat*.

Barry Morgan

The Most Rev'd Dr Barry Morgan has been a Bishop in the Church in Wales for 20 years and Archbishop for 10 years which he combines with being Bishop of Llandaff. He read History at London and Theology at Cambridge. He has published a number of articles and books, his latest being a study of the religious poetry of R.S. Thomas.

Osi Rhys Osmond

Originally from the Sirhowi Valley in Gwent, Osi Rhys Osmond is a painter, writer and cultural activist living in Llansteffan, Carmarthenshire. He has taught in the major Welsh art schools, exhibited internationally, broadcast and published in English and Welsh, is a member of the Welsh Arts Council and the Gorsedd of Bards and is represented in the National Library and National Museum of Wales art collections.

Alex Salmond
Alex Salmond MSP is the First Minister of Scotland.

M. Wynn Thomas
A Fellow of the British Academy and of the Learned Society of Wales, M. Wynn Thomas is Professor of English and Emyr Humphreys Professor of Welsh Writing in English at Swansea University. As editor of R.S. Thomas's unpublished estate he edited the posthumous volume *Residues* and recently published *R.S. Thomas: Serial Obsessive* (UWP, 2013).

Jeff Towns
Jeff Towns is a rare-book dealer based in Swansea who, for more than forty years, from his Dylans Bookstores in and around the city, has specialised in books about Wales in all its many aspects.

Encounters

with

DYLAN

edited by Jon Gower

To commemorate the centenary of another major Welsh poet and writer – and another Thomas – 2014 sees the publication of *Encounters with Dylan*, which will feature essays by academics and aficionados, poets and performers who have variously delighted in and engaged with the work of the self-styled 'Rimbaud of Cwmdonkin Drive'.

H'mm Foundation